Critical Guides to French Texts

102 Racine: Athalie

Critical Guides to French Texts

EDITED BY ROGER LITTLE, WOLFGANG VAN EMDEN, DAVID WILLIAMS

RACINE

Athalie

J. Dryhurst

Senior Lecturer in French
University of Leeds

Grant & Cutler Ltd
1994

© Grant & Cutler Ltd 1994

ISBN 0 7293 0369 1

1000438891

I.S.B.N. 84-401-2139-3

DEPÓSITO LEGAL: V. 524 - 1995

Printed in Spain by
Artes Gráficas Soler, S.A., Valencia
for
GRANT & CUTLER LTD
55–57 GREAT MARLBOROUGH STREET, LONDON W1V 2AY

Contents

Contents

Prefatory Note

The text of *Athalie* is readily available, both in editions of Racine's complete works, listed in the bibliography, and in separate editions, also listed there. I have used the one by R.-Y. Le Mazou, published in the Univers des Lettres series by Bordas, to which line numbers refer. Like other French editions aimed at *lycéens* and university students, it contains, in addition to the text of the play and its preface, biographical and other information on the author as well as copious notes and other helpful material. Italicised numbers in brackets in this book refer to numbered items in the bibliography at the end. For instance, the above edition is number (*6*). For a full biography of Racine, see Picard (*38*).

Introduction

Athalie is a play, and the primary purpose of most plays is to be acted. Reading them is second best, and should be seen as a preliminary to watching a future performance. Critical works exist, or should exist, therefore, in order to help audiences or potential audiences to understand and interpret the play in performance. The discussion of ideas — about the author's biography, philosophical ideas, dramatic theories, etc. — is interesting and important, but ultimately it all leads back to the stage. That stage, ideally, will be a physical one, but for many of us it will exist only in our mind and imagination. Nevertheless it is helpful, when reading a dramatic text, to have in mind the practical problems faced by the producer or the actor trying to interpret the text, such as: how old are the characters? how should they be dressed to reflect their age and character? what does this line mean and how should it be spoken? In the end, the play's indeed the thing and there is no substitute for it. It follows that this book is intended to be read with the text of the play to hand and, often, open, notably for the 'Plot' chapter.

In writing my book, I have had in mind sixth-form and university students, as well as other readers, who may not be particularly familiar with the French classical theatre and its conventions. At one time, French seventeenth-century plays were almost totally ignored by producers in Britain, being considered too static — legend had it that this was because there were no battles on stage, a serious omission for Shakespeare-lovers — but Molière, Racine, and even Corneille, usually in translation, are nowadays played in British theatres, both amateur and professional, as well as on television, and with increasing knowledge of the plays there is a greater willingness than before on the part of the public to accept their conventions.

Those conventions are in fact not particularly difficult to accept. The unities of time and place implied a maximum theoretical duration of twenty-four hours, and therefore a limited radius of travel. The unity of action meant that everything in the plot had to be related to, and to help to advance, the main action. Independent sub-plots were therefore inadmissible. The unities were in no way irksome for Racine and his contemporaries to accept; they were simply taken for granted.

So were the *bienséances*, which were of two kinds. *Bienséance intérieure* laid down that every work must be consonant with its own nature, e.g. that since tragedies are by definition tragic, they should not contain comic elements. *Bienséance extérieure* insisted that every work should be in conformity with its audience. The author must thus use language which the audience would consider appropriate to the subject and must not shock its sensibilities by portraying violence on stage. If this last were nevertheless to be done, it would also be most likely to offend the last of the rules, that of *vraisemblance*, since, apart from theoretical considerations, an audience which was used to public executions knew the difference between sham violence and the real thing.

When examined closely, the rules of the French classical theatre turn out in fact to be full of contradictions and quite arbitrary. Their effect in practice, however, is to concentrate the attention of the audience on what is essential. All that is extraneous to essentials is excluded, with physical action in particular being ruled out, since it generally serves only to distract the audience from the proper subject of the play, which is what goes on in the minds and, particularly in Racine's theatre, the hearts of the characters.

As to the language of *Athalie*, any problems it may pose for the new reader should not be great. Racine's vocabulary, in fact, is very small — some four thousand or so words — in comparison, say, with the tens of thousands of words employed by Shakespeare. Given such a small vocabulary, which he certainly did not see as a limitation, Racine used it in a way which is different from the techniques of English writers.

Images are few in number (and therefore more telling) and language is more abstract than in most English poets. Formality is the rule, but a formality which in Racine's hands produces grandeur rather than stiffness. The dignity of the style has to match the high dignity of the characters: Aristotle had advised that the characters of a tragedy should be of elevated status, so that the consequences of their actions would affect not only themselves but also those who depend on them. In the case of our play, as we shall see, the consequences of the downfall of the Queen and the safeguarding of the line of David affect the whole human race, giving Racine's observance of this rule in *Athalie* a very special character.

Some words in *Athalie* and other classical plays have a much stronger meaning than they have in modern French (e.g. *triste*, meaning *sombre*, *sévère*, and *ennui*, meaning *violent désespoir* — senses much closer to those of their Latin roots), but any decent edition will point these out. Perhaps the stylistic feature most liable to disconcert at first is the use of inversions, as in lines 5–6 of the play:

> ...Sitôt que de ce jour
> La trompette sacrée annonçait le retour

Here 'de ce jour' comes at the end of a line and before, rather than after, 'le retour'. Racine does this not only to avoid the ugly phrase 'le retour de ce jour' and to provide a rhyme but also to lay emphasis on the word 'jour' and on the particular day it represents — the feast of Pentecost. As well as the particular effects produced by the inversion, the general effect of using it is to add to the formal grandeur of the style. Here, as elsewhere, Racine, like other great writers, succeeds in killing a surprisingly large number of birds with an apparently limited number of stones.

I lay no claim to originality for this book. What is said in it comes mostly, consciously or unconsciously, from reading other critics and scholars. Some of them are referred to by name in the text. Details of their books and those of others are to be found in the Select Bibliography at the end. In many cases I may disagree, at least in part, with what they have to say and many of them disagree with each other, but to all of them I am greatly and humbly indebted for what they have taught me. When discussing the tragic nature of *Athalie*, for example, I have expressed disagreement with an idea put forward by the late Professor Odette de Mourgues in her excellent book, *Racine or the Triumph of Relevance (36)*, but it is only thanks to her idea that I have been able to suggest my own interpretation of the matter. I put forward my ideas in the hope of casting a little more light on a problem which she explored before me. If I have one aim above all for my book, it is to convey to, and share with, the reader a love and enthusiasm for French seventeenth-century literature and for Racine which I have in common with all my fellow workers and predecessors in the field.

As regards the spelling of biblical names, I have, for obvious reasons, used those of the characters in the play in their French form. By a happy chance they contain no accents, but since the name of Athalie's mother does not share that good fortune I have preferred to use the English form, Jezabel.

I should like to thank the many people who have helped me in the making of this book: the series Editors, Professor David Williams and Professor Wolfgang Van Emden, for their great patience and wise counsel; my colleagues, and in particular Dr David Coward, for their advice and encouragement and finally my wife, Patricia, for her constant help and support, physical, moral and intellectual, in bringing this work to fruition.

1. Origins

A little to the west of Versailles lies a small town called St-Cyr, now a dormitory suburb for Paris commuters, but best known in the late seventeenth century for an orphanage and school for the daughters of noble families. It had been founded by Mme de Maintenon, the widow of the poet Scarron, who had become the morganatic second wife of the ageing Louis XIV and had led him into more pious (but intolerant) ways than those of his youth. This was the unlikely place where *Athalie*, Racine's last play, was first performed.

The play, like the orphanage, was rather unusual. Racine, born in 1639, was himself an orphan, brought up from the age of three by his pious grandmother. She took him to live at the convent of Port-Royal, the centre of the Jansenist movement of which more will be said later but which for the moment is perhaps best characterised as a kind of French equivalent of the British Puritanism of the time. Nearby, there was a most unusual school, the *Petites Ecoles*, where he received an excellent classical education, developed a great love and knowledge of the Greek dramatists, and was imbued with Jansenist ideas. He was later to revolt, however, against his former masters and to scandalise them by winning fame and fortune in the professional theatre, only to leave it for the more desirable life of Historiographer Royal and courtier. The opportunity to do so came as a signal favour from the King, after the scandal surrounding the early performances of *Phèdre* in 1677. About the time of Racine's 'retirement' from the theatre there also began a process of reconciliation with his former friends and masters at Port-Royal, then the object of increasing persecution by the civil and religious authorities.

Twelve years later, in 1689, Mme de Maintenon interrupted the even tenor of his life at Court by 'requesting' him to write a play for the young *pensionnaires* of St-Cyr to act, a virtual command which it was impossible to refuse. The headmistress at St-Cyr, Mme Brinon, had already written pious plays for her pupils. These, however, were judged to be worthless. On the other hand, the girls' attempts at acting Racine's *Andromaque* had shown them as inclined to be rather too worldly-wise for Mme de Maintenon's taste. Something of greater literary worth than Mme Brinon's efforts, but more morally edifying than *Andromaque*, was needed. Hence the 'invitation' to Racine. The latter must have thought hard about being associated with the theatre again, given his previous life; professional players had a dubious social and moral reputation at the time and, indeed, were automatically excommunicated by the Church. Amateur dramatics, however, were respectable — indeed there was a long-standing tradition of educational drama in the Jesuit colleges, aimed at strengthening the boys' faith, their ability to speak in public and often, since that was the usual language of the plays, their Latin.

What Racine produced was a three-act play, *Esther*, a story taken from the Old Testament telling of the Jewish wife of the Persian emperor Assuérus, who persuaded him to end the persecution of her people. The play was a great success. In fact it turned out to be the highlight of two social seasons, running to many performances in the spring of 1689 and the winter of 1690. Courtiers vied for seats, the young *pensionnaires* were decked out in borrowed finery and jewels and acted and sang to the accompaniment of an orchestra playing music specially composed by Jean-Baptiste Moreau, St-Cyr's highly talented *maître de musique*. Indeed some contemporaries thought of *Esther* as being an opera, the genre which had lately come to rival tragedy in the public esteem, thanks to the works of a far better-known composer, Jean-Baptiste Lully. After this success, another 'request' soon followed. Racine once more chose an Old Testament subject, *Athalie*, and it was again Moreau who provided the musical score.

This time, however, there was no series of gala performances. In fact, although Racine and Moreau provided in *Athalie* the material for an even more splendid production than *Esther*, it did not even have a proper performance in its author's lifetime. Indeed the nearest that the new play came to being performed was early in 1691, but in the form of a few *répétitions*, rather than *représentations*, at St-Cyr and at Versailles. At most, if not all, of them there was a harpsichord instead of an orchestra. There were no elaborate costumes and the performers played in small rooms and in private, albeit before the King and important guests such as the deposed James II of England and his queen.

The reasons for this 'stifling' of *Athalie* have been the cause of much spilt ink. J. Orcibal (*37*) sees the explanation in contemporary politics. For him Racine's play is a kind of allegory figuring the unjust deposition and hoped-for restoration of James II, replaced on the throne of England by the usurper William of Orange, the great enemy of Louis XIV.

This view of the matter is opposed by R. Picard (*38*, p.148), among others. He, rightly in my view, sees the 'toning down' of the performances of *Athalie* as being due rather to the criticisms of certain ecclesiastics, and notably those of Hébert, the parish priest of Versailles. Hébert shared the anti-theatre prejudices of many, though not all, church people of his time. For him, *Esther* had been turned into a means of leading the young ladies into temptation by flaunting themselves on the stage rather than serving as a means of edifying them through the words they were given to speak or sing. He, and others, were determined that *Athalie* should not be allowed to do the same, and Mme de Maintenon, and indeed the King himself, was obliged to yield to ecclesiastical pressure and abandon the project. Racine's compensation was his appointment, in December 1690, as *gentilhomme ordinaire* to the King, a very special honour which made him the envy of many at court. Moreover, when *Athalie* was printed, in the early spring of 1691, the *privilège* authorising its publication made it clear that it had been 'composée par ordre du Roi'.

Whatever the reasons for Racine's choosing the story of Athalie for his play, it has struck many as being a strange choice. Two possible reasons for it are clear: Joas, like the *pensionnaires* and moreover Racine himself, was an orphan and Louis XIV had been a boy king — indeed, at five years old he had been younger than Joas when he succeeded his father in 1643. Apart from that, the bloodthirstiness of *Athalie* makes it a surprising subject for a play to be acted by supposedly refined and sensitive young ladies.

Racine found his subject in II Kings 11, 12 (a parallel account is in II Chronicles 22–24) and in the Jewish historian Josephus. The ninth century B.C. was a savage period in Jewish history. The Chosen People had split into two kingdoms, Israel and Juda, with vicious rivalries between kingdoms and dynasties. The religious leaders and prophets strove to keep the people faithful to the Law and the one God in face of the fertility cults of Baal and Astarte. Occasionally they would find a new leader to come forward in the name of the Almighty in order to punish, and sometimes replace, a particularly wicked one.

Thus Jehu had deposed Ahab's son Jehoram (the Joram of Racine's text) and massacred Athalie's mother, Jezabel, and all their family. Athalie responded by killing, as she thought, all the heirs to the kingdom of Juda — her own grandchildren — only to be killed herself after entering the Temple. Like many other happenings in Kings, it is an uncompromisingly barbaric story, apparently fired by a mixture of religious fanaticism and dynastic rivalry. The one often serves as a pretext for the other, no quarter is given or asked, and there are the usual interventions by God from time to time to make a terrible example of His enemies. Bossuet (9) had quoted it as an example of the fate of wicked rulers and it had earlier been the subject of an obscure, not to say strange, college play of 1658 of which H.C. Lancaster (27, p.303) gives details.

The accounts in Kings and Chronicles (the latter known in French as *Paralipomènes*) gave Racine the basic story and the main characters: Joas, Joad, Josabet, Zacharie, Athalie and Mathan. To these he added Abner, whom Joad uses to help induce Athalie to enter the Temple (she enters spontaneously in the Bible) and the *confidents*. We also owe to Racine the setting at Pentecost (particularly significant, as I hope to show), Joad's prophecy and, of course, all the subtle psychology of the characters and his own incomparable poetry.

Another important source is the Greek theatre, and in particular Euripides, beloved of Racine since his schooldays at Port-Royal and a constant influence on his plays, several of which are based directly on Greek sources. The subject of *Athalie* is, of course, not Greek. However, scenes from the *Io* of Euripides lie behind both Athalie's interrogation of young Joas (II.7) and the 'moral' which ends the play, as R.C. Knight (*26*, p.388) has pointed out. The use of a chorus, unusual for Racine's time, is also Greek in origin. The chorus had been a feature of plays by some sixteenth-century dramatists, such as Garnier's *Les Juifves*, a biblical play whose choruses, like those of *Athalie*, draw deeply on the Psalms.[1] The device had been dropped by seventeenth-century dramatists, perhaps because it might be thought of as slowing up the action.

In using a chorus in *Athalie*, Racine was thus returning to the Greek tradition. Yet it is not so much the use of Greek forms but above all the whole spirit of a play which is deeply religious as well as profoundly human in character which brings Racine closer to the ancient tragedies than almost any other writer.

One final 'source' of this, his last play, was Racine's long experience of the theatre. *Athalie*, like Beethoven's Ninth Symphony, came at the end of a long career writing for critical audiences. Both works stand apart as masterpieces through the willingness of each artist to experiment with form (both works, incidentally, going against contemporary fashion in using a chorus), with a confidence born of past achievements.

The production problems of *Athalie* also set it apart, either delighting or daunting the producer according to the resources he has at his disposal, since the unusually large cast, the elaborate Temple setting and, in particular, Moreau's magnificent music cannot always be adequately reproduced. If some contemporaries spoke of *Esther* as being an opera, *Athalie* is emphatically not an opera. The atmosphere of Moreau's overture and choruses may perhaps make one think at times of an oratorio, but their real effect is the one for which they were clearly intended: to enhance and

---

[1] I am grateful to Professor Van Emden for drawing this point to my attention.

confirm the beauty and grandeur of Racine's tragedy. Many audiences have to be content with spoken choruses; indeed the first public performance in 1716 omitted them altogether. Nowadays, at least, recordings are available to remind us of what Racine and Moreau hoped to do, even if their hopes were frustrated at the time, and to give us an idea of the total theatrical experience which a full production can evoke.

2. The Plot: a Commentary

Aristotle, in his *Poetics* (*12*, p.40), declared that he could envisage a play without characters (i.e. fully developed characters) but not one without a plot, for it would then lack the main constituent of drama, which is action. Racine defined his ideal for this in the first preface to *Britannicus* as 'une action simple, chargée de peu de matière' and illustrated it to the most striking degree in *Bérénice*. Indeed few of Racine's plays have so slim a plot as this story of the parting of a Roman emperor and a Palestinian queen, who cannot marry because of the Roman prejudice against royalty.

The plot of *Athalie*, however, is very different from that of *Bérénice*, which has been seen by some critics as archetypal Racine, a plot made of next to nothing. *Athalie* has much more in common with Racine's last great 'secular' play, *Phèdre*. In the latter play the background to the action is important to a full appreciation of its consequences: the family history of Phèdre, the unexpected return of the wandering Theseus, the relationships of both spouses with the gods, etc. In *Athalie*, too, the surrounding circumstances are important and more than a little complex. It also contains more open violence than Racine's other plays, whose threats tend to be hidden, as in *Britannicus*, where Néron spies on Junie's interview with Britannicus, or in *Bajazet*, where the protagonists are under constant threat of strangulation by the *muets*, the hidden guards of the Sultan's harem. Perhaps Racine thought that his young actresses would be able to cope better with violence of a more blood-and-thunder kind than with such nightmare-inducing predicaments.

Certainly the plot of *Athalie* is exciting and full of suspense. We would not, of course, expect suspense to be the main feature of a play which seeks to explore the human condition rather than merely to excite the spectator. Yet suspense is important dramatically in *Athalie*. It is not, however, artificially contrived. It is brought about by the natural behaviour of the characters, and often by the unpredictability of Athalie, who has, before the start of the play, been a predictably efficient tyrant. She starts with total superiority over her opponents, but mistakes which are quite untypical of her bring about the reversal of fortune which marks her downfall and the triumph of Joas.

The action begins with Abner's firm monosyllable, *Oui*. Incidentally, two of Racine's other plays, *Andromaque* and *Iphigénie*, begin in the same way. It is a practical device which serves both to hush the audience and to bring it into the middle of an ongoing conversation. Here, however, the word is also highly significant for the plot: it symbolises and expresses Abner's willingness to side with God rather than Athalie. When the play reaches its end, it is this willingness which determines the final outcome and all of its far-reaching consequences.

Abner also informs us that it is Pentecost, the feast when the Jewish people celebrate the day when God gave Moses the Ten Commandments, the basis of His Law, and made the Covenant by which He accepted them as His chosen people. Significantly also, it is a feast of justice and peace, whose past celebrations Abner contrasts with those of the present one, held at a time when faithful Jews are being unjustly persecuted by the violent usurper Athalie — the rhymes at lines 59–60, 'sanguinaire' and 'sanctuaire', say all — and the reference to Athalie's mother Jezabel underlines the typically Racinian theme of malevolent heredity. Her murder of her grandchildren, the last descendants of David, has apparently frustrated God's promise of a Messiah, so the future prospects for the Jewish people seem to be as bleak as the present ones. It seems that the play might as well not continue.

Abner's forbidding portrait of Athalie includes a significant detail concerning her lust for gold (I.1.48–50) and an allusion to 'des trésors par David amassés' which prepare the spectator for her later fatal willingness to enter the Temple virtually unescorted (V.5.1715). In the face of Abner's pessimism, however, Joad still strongly proclaims his own faith in God. He cleverly works on Abner's conscience and self-confidence so as to ensure his practical co-operation when the moment comes, and with his roundabout hint (153) and the clear command to Abner to be at the Temple later that morning, the scene ends on a note of mystery and hope. The reference to dawn (160) symbolises this hope, as well as being a subtle reminder of the unity of time.

As we first meet Josabet (I.2), the tension begins to increase: Athalie is planning to worship Baal in the Temple itself, the ultimate sacrilege. Joad's mysterious hint to Abner is now explained: young Joas, the rightful heir to the throne, is alive, and he must now be declared king as soon as possible. Josabet, in a dramatically ironic reply to Joad (I.2.235–40), renews the heredity theme by wondering whether the boy can avoid the fate of his tainted family: he is, after all, descended from Athalie and Jezabel. Joad echoes these fears in his prayer (I.2.283–86) that Joas should be like 'le fruit en naissant arraché' rather than 'de David abandonner la trace'. This prayer raises some interesting questions. God does not answer it, in the sense that Joad is crowned during the play and was later to be unfaithful to God and to have Joad's son, his childhood companion Zacharie, murdered. Yet the prayer is answered by the fact that Joas does continue the all-important line of David, who himself had at times been unfaithful to God, and ensure the coming of the Messiah. So even imperfect human beings can still serve the Almighty, who clearly knows better than the perfectionist Joad.

Next Josabet recounts the terrible scene from which she rescued the infant Joas. This prefigures and contrasts with the later and more famous *songe d'Athalie* by reminding us of the Queen's murderous record and of the immediate threat she poses. It also brings Joad to speak of his plans. Although he constantly reiterates his trust in the Almighty, Joad is also a practical realist and his plans take account of the popular appeal of the young and innocent Joas in comparison with the horrid daughter of Jezabel. There is an important moment of dramatic irony when Joad prays (292) that God will induce his enemies to make a mistake, a reminder of a familiar Latin proverb: *Quos deus vult perdere prius dementat* ('Those whom a god wants to destroy, he first makes mad') which the plot later fulfils. With the exposition now complete — we know the situation, although we have yet to meet Joas and Athalie — Joad goes to prepare for the Pentecost ceremonies while a chorus of great poetic beauty emphasises the contrast between the violence and injustice of Athalie's régime and the Law, based on love, which Moses received at the first Pentecost, whose anniversary is about to be celebrated.

Act II follows immediately on Act I, for there are no intervals in *Athalie*, the action being continuous, and Josabet and Salomith remain on stage with the chorus. This continuity could have presented a problem on the professional stage, where acts did not exceed about twenty-five minutes in length because of the need to trim the wicks of the candles. No doubt lighting facilities were better at Court. The chorus is interrupted by Zacharie entering to announce, in a *coup de théâtre* (I.2.396), that Athalie has made a sacrilegious intrusion into the sacred Temple. (It must not be forgotten, in this context, that blasphemy and sacrilege were considered as heinous offences and punishable by death in seventeenth-century France.)

Athalie herself then enters, but she is not the fierce and defiant tyrant we have been led to expect. Described by Zacharie just before she enters as dumbstruck by the sight of Joas, she appears in the flesh as a downcast, apparently weak and worried woman, in search of 'Cette paix qu'[elle] cherche et qui [la] fuit toujours' (II.3.435). She feels compelled to make a kind of public confession, trying to justify her past conduct by its present political results. Then, regaining some courage, she vaunts her achievements (we notice her constant use of the first person singular), mentioning in particular Jehu, who had killed her mother in Yahweh's name and who now 'tremble dans Samarie' (II.5.480), an initial expression of the pride which she displays increasingly as the play progresses.

Next, however, she tells, in horrifyingly realistic language, very different from Racine's usual elegant paraphrases, of her terrible dream (II.5). We share her horror, sympathising with her longing for peace and forgetting her past (despite Josabet's recent reminder of it in I.2), and we even begin to feel sorry for her. Yet her recognition of Joas as the child who stabbed her in the dream (as she, incidentally, had stabbed him in real life) renews our fears for him, earlier expressed by Josabet (II.2.421). These fears are redoubled when the unscrupulous Mathan, predictably, counsels killing him on the mere suspicion that he constitutes a threat. Athalie, perhaps for her own comfort, prefers to believe Abner's reassurance, but still sends for the child, to the horror of the audience.

When she orders the discreet mobilisation of her troops, she seems to be her old self and in control of the situation again (II.6), but is horrified (II.7) when she becomes certain that Joas is the child in her dream. Yet his simplicity and innocence strike in her an unaccustomed chord of pity. This reaction momentarily regains our sympathy and, perhaps, explains her unexpected use of the respect-ful *vous* to him. Another moment of great dramatic irony comes as Abner (II.7.657–58) almost teasingly identifies Athalie's pity with the *coup fatal* she fears from Joas and which she later actually receives because of him.

Racine once more shows his mastery of dramatic suspense and of character when, as Josabet starts to lead Joas away, the tension relaxes, only to rise quickly again when Athalie makes him stay, perhaps out of curiosity, perhaps from suspicion. All eyes are now concentrated on the young Joas in this unequal and dramatically compelling encounter, but he stands firm and provokes her rage by professing his faith in a God who rewards the virtuous and punishes the wicked. Controlling herself once more, Athalie tries to seduce the boy from his life of austerity in the Temple, seeing his previous replies as mere echoes of the teaching of Joad and Josabet, but his most cutting reply, 'Quel père/Je quitterais! Et pour ... quelle mère!' (699–700) is surely his own.

Athalie's subsequent anger leads her to defend the murder of her grandchildren and to express her hatred for the Jewish God. Indeed she taunts Him (734), in a challenge which expands on her earlier boast of having tamed Jehu (II.5.480) and is a high point in the epic duel between her and Yahweh which forms such a feature of the play. She defies Him to produce the promised Messiah now that, as she believes, she has destroyed the line of David. The dramatic irony which underlines — and undermines — this supreme expression of her pride is, of course, the fact that Joas is still safe, as Abner soon reminds us. With Joad standing guard in the wings, the act has been centred around Joas and Athalie, with Josabet, the former's rescuer, providing a striking contrast with the cruel queen. It comes to an end with the chorus debating as to which of the two will prevail.

The third act, like the second, begins with a *coup de théâtre* as Mathan and Nabal smugly enter the Temple, bearing an order for Josabet from Athalie. After some untypical wavering, she is now demanding Joas as a hostage. The audience senses that the tide is again running in her favour and Mathan savours the seemingly inevitable victory which is to come (III.3). When Josabet arrives, he drops his bombshell. Once again all seems lost and indeed his crafty questioning almost forces her to reveal the child's identity (III.4), but she is saved by a strange kind of divine intervention when Mathan's allusion to her God provokes her to an angry riposte. Then Joad arrives (III.5) and, in a great dramatic reversal, withers Mathan with terrifying invective.

The odds, previously heavily loaded against Joad, now seem at last to be changing: with both Athalie and Mathan in apparent disarray we feel that he has some chance of winning, even though only the Levites and the chorus remain to defend the Temple. The significance of the moment is emphasised by Joad's prophecy (III.7), foretelling the death of his own son Zacharie at the hand of Joas, the destruction of Jerusalem and the coming of a new Jerusalem under the Messiah: in spite of appearances, good will finally prevail over evil. Racine in his preface admits that the prophecy is an episode, not contributing directly to the advancement of the play's action and thus, strictly speaking, infringing the unity of action. In practice, however, by the power of its poetry it serves to underline the importance of that action and of its epic scope, placing the events of the play in the perspective of the history of the whole human race.

Immediately after his interval of prophetic ecstasy, Joad moves into action. He orders the royal crown to be prepared and the Levites to arm themselves. With the plot moving towards its climax, the chorus echoes the audience's fears for the final outcome and proclaims its wonderment, as participant in the action, at the significance of these preparations and of Joad's prophecy.

A procession opens Act Four, theatrically effective in that it is both solemn and homely. Joas enters with the High Priest's family, in which he has been brought up. He is, however, preceded by the symbols of kingship: David's sword, the crown and the Book of the Law. Josabet tries the crown on the head of the boy, who then runs, in a touching gesture, into the arms of his foster-father. The latter next formally questions him (IV.2) about his loyalty to God and the duties of a king. This formal examination marks the end of Joas's education for kingship — not a very successful one, perhaps, in the light of his future killing of Zacharie and of other misdeeds he was later to commit — and reminds us, as does the reference to the duc de Bourgogne in the preface, of the importance attached to the education of princes in Racine's day. In the same context, it is perhaps useful also to remember the effect that the first two scenes of this act, even in a simple *répétition*, must have had at St-Cyr, with the self-conscious young actresses processing and the charming contrast they created with the formal real-life ceremonial of the Court of Louis XIV.

To return to the plot, Joad next prostrates himself in homage before the startled child, whom he addresses for the first time as Joas and presents (IV.2) to the chief Levites. This presentation of the young king to the Levites is important, firstly because it formally establishes his right to rule and secondly because it raises the standard of battle, now that there is a king to fight for. So the mood of the drama changes from solemnity to preparation for war and the tension rises yet higher. Joad addresses the chief Levites like the good general he is, emphasising their advantages over the enemy: surprise and high motivation. Having secured their allegiance, he knows that his preparations are complete, and there is time for an extraordinary expression of affection and tenderness for Joas by the

High Priest. There is also a moment of high dramatic irony (IV.4) as Joas embraces Zacharie, whom Joad had prophesied (III.7.1143) he was later to kill. The momentary relaxation of tension is, however, soon interrupted. With the announcement that the Temple is surrounded, the mechanism of the plot is fully wound. The act ends with the Levites taking up their posts and Joas leaving to be crowned as the chorus invokes God's assistance.

We do not see the coronation itself, with its semi-sacramental anointing of the king. Besides interrupting the action, the portrayal on stage of such a sacred ceremony would have been unseemly. In fact Zacharie's *récit*, which opens Act V, paints the scene far better. The momentary peace it brings from the crisis is, however, soon shattered. Athalie's troops are at the gates and Abner suddenly arrives (V.2) with an ultimatum from her. He describes her as having 'un air égaré', obsessed by the desire to see and possess the mysterious boy and, more particularly, King David's treasure. He also emphasises what we already know of — her deep and pathological hatred for the Jewish God and, given his ignorance of the boy's true identity, gives what seems to be the only sensible advice: to comply with her demands.

All again seems lost and Joad has his back to the wall. He needs both a moment to think and the reassurance of Abner's ultimate loyalty. He gets the first while receiving the second and then gives Abner his answer: Athalie may enter the Temple, escorted, but not by a pillaging army. Abner will then judge if the boy should be handed over. This reply of Joad's, sometimes attacked as hypocritical, will be discussed later. Dramatically it represents a moment of high tension and suspense, soon to be followed by others.

Athalie is now (V.5) in the Temple, believing that her moment of triumph has come. She marks this ultimate moment of overweening pride by contemptuously greeting the High Priest, using the *tu* form. But with the gate locked securely behind her, the moment of truth has come and Joad needs but few words for his reply before the curtains fall away in a truly magnificent *coup de théâtre* to reveal the young king. Athalie and Abner are thunderstruck, but Athalie's subsequent anger, as she confidently calls on her escort to kill the boy, turns to horror when the hidden Levites appear: 'Ô trahison, ô reine infortunée!' (1731). The last three words may appear to be a mere oratorical cliché, yet they ring surprisingly true: indeed the cry of treason is recorded in the Bible and people in dire situations can find it difficult above all to admit to themselves that a disaster has actually happened to them. Coming to her senses, Athalie finds her courage again, first turning in vain to Abner, then thinking of her army outside, only to learn that it has fled and that Mathan is dead.

Her final admission of defeat marks her reversal of fortune in the drama, and its contemptuous 'tu l'emportes!' (1768), is both an acknowledgement and a defiance of her victor, the Jewish God. She likewise acknowledges Joas as king, but only to curse him with the wish that her grandchild will come to resemble herself. Joad promptly orders her execution and she is dragged away to her death (off-stage, of course). Joas prays (V.7), in yet another moment of dramatic irony, underlining the theme of heredity, that her curse may not come true, although the audience knows that it will, just as Joad has prophesied. Peace and order finally return with Joad (V.8) proclaiming God's concern for the weak and the innocent and insisting in the last line of the play that he is, appropriately for both the young Joas and the young actresses of St-Cyr, '[pour] l'orphelin un père'.

It has already been mentioned that the ending of the play, with its 'moral', echoes a Greek source, the *Io* of Euripides. Another obvious source is Corneille's *Rodogune*, where Cléopâtre, having taken the poison she had intended for her son Antiochus and his bride Rodogune, expresses the wish that they may have 'un fils qui [lui] ressemble' (*Rodogune*, V.4.1824). Added to the fact that Antiochus had earlier suspected his bride of preparing the poison, this considerably darkens the prospects for the future of their marriage. The ending of Racine's play is ultimately far less pessimistic, however. Even though we know that Athalie's curse will come true, yet Joad's closing speech reminds us that God is concerned for the fate of the weak and the innocent and that evil will not have the last word.

3. Characters: Athalie

Racine's problem with Athalie is very similar to Milton's with Satan in *Paradise Lost*. The hero — the main character — of an epic or tragedy must not be so totally innocent that we are scandalised at his fate, yet he must be virtuous enough to excite some sympathy. Otherwise, as Aristotle pointed out (*12*, p.48), we will feel that his punishment is well deserved. So what sympathy can we feel for a character of ill repute like Athalie or, *a fortiori*, for Satan, who is the very source and focus of evil throughout the whole of creation?

Wicked heroes or heroines were not unknown in the French classical theatre, as we have just seen with Corneille's Cléopâtre in *Rodogune*. What Corneille was concerned with gaining for her, however, was not sympathy, but what he called *admiration*. This could be summarised as wonderment at the possibilities of human nature which were expressed in her very wickedness, an idea to which we shall return later. Racine, who did not share Corneille's views on the aims of tragedy in this respect, had already faced the problem of the wicked hero earlier in his career, notably when portraying Néron, the principal male character, if not the nominal hero, of his *Britannicus*. Yet, in contrast with Athalie, Néron, the so-called 'monstre naissant', is a young man of previously good character who is starting to go spectacularly to the bad but is not obviously wicked at the beginning of the play. Perhaps because of this fact, his presence does not loom quite as large as that of Athalie, despite the relative brevity of her part (she appears only in Acts II and V). Athalie, then, is clearly wicked. Moreover, even if Racine had wanted to portray her differently, the Athalie of the Bible was there to contradict him and he could not have changed the facts of the Bible to any great extent without being accused of heresy as well as of inaccuracy.

He goes some way towards solving his difficulty by presenting Athalie, as we have seen, not as the ruthless tyrant she normally is, but as a weak and emotional human being. Her dream, the horrendous vision of her mother Jezabel and the seemingly innocent child who stabs her to the heart, has left her in a pitiful state, prompting Mathan to ask her 'Quel trouble vous agite?' (II.5.460). We are not allowed to forget, however, that this state is of very recent origin and her habitual arrogance shows through when she defends her past conduct to Abner and Josabet (II.5.467–83, II.7.709). 'Le Ciel même a pris soin de me justifier', she declares and she boasts of the 'éclatants succès' on which her power is based (470–71). Yet Racine does soften her implacable image and underlines his effect by portraying her opponents, notably Joad and even Yahweh Himself, as harsh and unsympathetic, at least in their dealings with her.

Yet can anything positive really be said in Athalie's favour? One of her earliest defenders was Voltaire (*46*) in a prefatory *Discours* to his play *Les Guèbres*, in which he praises religious toleration by presenting *Athalie* as a story of fanaticism run rife, with Joad as the main guilty party and Athalie as his victim, an almost benevolent centenarian queen in search of an heir to her throne and who sees the young Eliacin/Joas as a suitable candidate. Perhaps Voltaire formed this impression of her character from the way he had seen the part played. Certainly a reading of either the Bible or Racine's play, whatever impression it may give of Joad, clearly suggests a much younger, more vigorous and less well-intentioned Athalie, whose past record is as hard to defend as her present conduct.

Her record really is sinister, however cleverly she tries to justify it on political grounds. Abner, who has faithfully served both her and her son and predecessor Ochosias, is under no misapprehensions about her. His accusations, dispersed throughout the first scene of the play, include violence, enmity to goodness and justice, wickedness, the lust for gold, haughtiness, anger, bloodthirstiness, etc. Joad, more biased but none the less factual, adds, in the same scene, the adjectives 'regicidal', 'parricidal', 'usurping', 'perfidious', 'criminal', etc. Of all her deeds the most horrible is, of course, the murder of her grandchildren: if she could kill them, she could do anything, and Josabet's eye-witness account of 'l'implacable Athalie', dagger in hand, leaves us in no doubt about her ruthlessness. The defence that 'Ce que j'ai fait, Abner, j'ai cru le devoir faire' (II.5.467) is unconvincing: however well the country was governed, with peace at home and on the frontiers, was a roomful of slaughtered children, and her own flesh and blood at that, necessary to bring it about?

We are naturally driven to wonder about the motive for this ghastly deed. Was it lust for power? The desire for vengeance? Religious fanaticism, so that Baal might triumph over Yahweh? Or a mixture of these reasons? The Bible account (II Kings 11.1) is vague: 'Now when Athaliah the mother of Ahaziah [Ochosias] learned that her son was dead, she promptly did away with all those of royal stock'. Racine's preface to *Athalie* is a little more explicit: 'Athalie, ayant appris à Jérusalem tous ces massacres, entreprit de son côté d'éteindre entièrement la race royale de David'. Clearly a key element is Athalie's deep enmity towards the house of David, but what is the reason for this and for the murders?

Stung to anger at the end of her interrogation of Joas (II.7), she justifies the murder firstly by her 'juste fureur' at Jehu's massacre of her parents, her brother and eighty other princes. All these relatives were killed, as she says, 'Pour venger je ne sais quels prophètes' (715), executed by her mother for their 'fureurs indiscrètes'. These 'prophets', according to modern scholarship, as evidenced by the Jerusalem Bible (8, note to I Samuel 10.5), would in fact seem to have been more akin to Egyptian dervishes than to the great prophets like Elijah, but Racine's use of 'indiscrètes' suggests that they had criticised Jezabel's conduct. To have failed to respond in kind to Jehu's 'aveugle rage' (719) would have meant for Athalie that she was cowardly, unfaithful to her parents' memory, and 'esclave d'une lâche et frivole pitié' (718). Incidentally, her brutal reaction here helps us to understand why she had been so surprised earlier in the scene (654) at the idea of feeling pity for Eliacin/Joas. At the same time her account of Jehu's barbarity towards her family fills us with great revulsion for him. Yet even on the basis of an eye for an eye, it does not excuse Athalie's murder of her grandchildren.

An examination of what she says would thus seem to suggest that among her reasons for the murders were an atavistic loyalty to her own blood-line, the fear of being thought cowardly (and hence, no doubt, for a woman living in those times, of seeming politically unreliable) and total incomprehension of the prophet's criticisms of the crimes of her mother, Jezabel. She also puts forward the motive of pure self-interest: 'Où serais-je aujourd'hui?' (723) and finally, and perhaps most significantly, that of hatred of the Jewish God and all who support him, declaring that the 'implacable vengeance' of Yahweh has made the house of David an object of horror and enmity for her (729–30).

It is very clear from all this that Athalie places self-interest, in all its forms, above everything and everyone else. By implication, this idea justified, for instance, her mother's contriving of the murder of Naboth in order to steal his vineyard (I Kings 21) and it explains also the willingness even to murder her own grandchildren for personal revenge and for fear of being thought weak and losing power. We hear no mention from Athalie of the monarch's duties to her people, let alone to the weak and helpless. She is totally wrapped up in herself. She may have been close to her mother, but she is quite oblivious of others and her ultimate selfishness is invincible; she acts out of a kind of inevitability, because she is who she is. One thinks of her genetic inheritance — in Racine's preface she is 'fille d'Achab et de Jézabel' just as Phèdre is 'La fille de Minos et de Pasiphaë'. One of the chaplains at Port-Royal, Isaac Lemaître de Saci, passed the following judgement on her:

> ...née dans une maison toute remplie d'impiété et de cruauté [Athalie] avait sucé avec le lait cette amertume criminelle du péché. Elle s'en était toujours nourrie depuis. Et ainsi un cœur tout abandonné au crime ne pouvait produire, selon l'Evangile, que des fruits de

mort. (Bible dite de Saci, t.XI, 2e éd., 562, quoted by
Orcibal, *37* p.94, n.29)

Athalie is, as we have seen, not alone in her savage behaviour. For
Jehu as for her, genocide is a recognised means of settling disputes.
The modern spectator may thus find it hard to distinguish between
her and her fanatical opponents, but there is a difference, symbol-
ised by Pentecost, the feast around which the play is centred and
which celebrates the giving of the Law and its ten commandments.
These forbade crimes like murder and stealing and laid down a
basis for civilised life by defining the rights of others. The punishment meted out by Jehu may have been barbaric, but it was not
arbitrary, for it was seen as being carried out by divine order and in
retaliation for Jezabel's flouting of the Law and of justice. For her,
as for her daughter Athalie, the only ultimate yardstick was
constituted by her own arbitrary desires; so long as they were
attained, other people were expendable.

Athalie's values, then, seem as unattractive as the character
which they underlie. Since her troubled state partly obscures this
fact, Racine's basic problem of gaining real sympathy for her would
still seem to remain. Yet, at the end of the play, especially when she
utters her famous cry, 'Dieu des Juifs, tu l'emportes' (V. 6. 1768),
we do feel genuinely sorry for her. Why? Perhaps it is because at
that point she is a fellow human being, crushed by a power far
superior to her own, yet admitting defeat only at the last. Like
Milton's Satan (who is, of course, not human), she is one 'Who
durst defy the Omnipotent to arms', and despite what they both
stand for, we still have a sneaking regard for their defiance: their
characters may be grim, but so are their respective fates, and they
both go down fighting. Our ultimate attitude to them is based not on
a careful weighing up of their values and behaviour but on a gut
reaction which is very revealing as far as human nature is
concerned.

Corneille, as was mentioned above, explained the attraction of
evil characters by what he called *admiration*, in the Latin sense of
the word, meaning 'amazement' or 'wonderment'. Faced with a

powerful but evil character, the spectator is brought up against some
of the less desirable but real and extraordinary possibilities of
human nature and, while condemning that character's evil actions,
may yet 'admirer la source dont elles partent' (*Rodogune, Préface*).
This is not, of course, to imply even for a moment that such was
Racine's intention with Athalie or to suggest that our reaction is
only or necessarily one of wonderment. Yet Corneille's idea does
offer clues towards an explanation of this puzzling aspect of human
behaviour: indeed wonderment can be mixed with, or lead on to,
pity and sympathy for a wicked character who is *in extremis*. It does
not stop us from rejoicing at the ending of the career of wickedness,
and it is perhaps not quite the Christian idea of hating the sin but
loving the sinner. Yet certainly in the case of Athalie our feelings
are not all negative, despite her crimes and Aristotle's strictures on
wicked heroes. We cannot condone her behaviour, yet finally we do
both pity her plight and, to some extent, admire her courage,
however misplaced, since both are aspects of the human condition
which we all share. In particular, the final sight of a fellow human
being about to be dragged off to her death makes us forget, at least
at that instant, the crimes which brought her death about.

   Athalie's adversary is Yahweh, the God of her own subjects,
the Jews. She clearly admits His existence throughout the play and
confesses His power at the end, but at no point does she acknowledge His authority, as Joad feels she should. Yet she is not portrayed
as an honest and moral follower of Baal, the god of her home
country of Tyre, or shown as wrongly condemned by Joad and his
party for not rejecting that deity in order to worship a God in whom
she cannot believe. She was, it is true, going to the temple of Baal to
pray him to 'veiller sur [sa] vie' (II.5.524) when 'un instinct' urged
her to go to that of Yahweh, to the great consternation of its inhabitants. However, she certainly bears no resemblance to the honest
unbeliever whom Pascal was trying to lead towards faith: '…je ne
suis pas en liberté, on ne me relâche pas et je suis fait de telle sorte
que je ne puis pas croire' (*Pensées*, No. 418, Lafuma text; No. 233,
Brunschvicg text). She is no earnest seeker after truth and, *pace*
Voltaire, certainly no apostle of tolerance. As Abner, perhaps the

most tolerant character in the whole play, points out when she bursts into the Temple, she is certainly lacking in respect for the religion of the country of which she is queen. For Joad, however, she is wicked not only because of her evil deeds but also because she refuses to accept Yahweh as the one true God. For him, these two facts are interdependent: her problem is as much one of faith as of morals: indeed her moral depravity stems from her refusal to accept, or at least to respect, Yahweh.

In practice, however, Athalie seems to see gods, whoever they may be, mainly as forces to be reckoned with in the power game, whose wrath may be forestalled by the taking out of a kind of insurance policy. Thus she explains to Mathan (II.5.523) why she had gone into the Temple: she had been about to go and pray to Baal to grant her peace of mind when the thought occurred to her to try and appease Yahweh. This, together with her pity for Joas (II.7.654) may give us the idea of a possible 'conversion' of Athalie to better behaviour, but her previous record and character make this most improbable, certainly without a miracle of a kind unheard of in Racine. Ultimately it is on herself alone that Athalie relies when contesting with Yahweh, and the fact that human beings are no match for gods wins for her at least some of our pity and sympathy.

Seen in the light of its principal character, then, *Athalie* is a tale of defiance of the supreme power by a mere human being. However, we must remember that Athalie's defiance of Yahweh has a wider, epic dimension, contained explicitly in the cruel taunt she makes to the dignified Josabet (II.7.734) about the impossibility of the promised Messiah's coming now that the murder of her grandchildren has, as she thinks, destroyed the line of David. To this one might add the boast which Abner reports her as making to him (V.2.1580) as she stands with her soldiers outside the Temple, threatening to burn it down, 'Et ton Dieu contre moi ne le saurait défendre'. This boast is blasphemous, and similar ones are to be found in medieval literature (e.g. Cain in the *Jeu d'Adam*, Raoul de Cambrai), made at moments of total *desmesure*. [2] Such a direct and specific challenge to a god in a tragedy must be answered, and it is

---

[2] I am grateful to Professor Van Emden for drawing my attention to this.

in *Athalie*. But her challenge is a very special one. It involves a threatened change in the very course of history by the frustration of God's plans for the salvation of mankind through the Messiah, who was to bring a reign of peace and justice for the whole human race. No challenge could be greater and her ambitions and her overweening pride are on the grandest of scales. Yet they finally blind her, as Joad hopes and foresees, to the true identity of Eliacin and thus bring about her destruction. Clearly the duel between Athalie and the Almighty can have only one ending, but grandeur is certainly not lacking either in the play or in its main protagonist.

4. Characters: Joad

Joad's part is both long (he is on stage nearly all the time) and unusual — Old Testament prophets are rare in the theatre and, since the prophet's task is to show people the error of their ways, such characters are liable to appear unsympathetic to the audience. Joad does not speak merely on his own account. As a prophet he is the principal spokesman in the play for Yahweh Himself, the invisible character whose presence dominates the whole action, and he is also the main representative of the values of his religion, many of which values the play was no doubt commissioned to expound.

The view of God which Joad projects, however, is, on the whole, an off-putting one. Unlike the choruses, which sing of a bounteous and loving God whose constant care is for the human race, and in particular for the weak and defenceless, he more often speaks of a jealous deity whose principal concern seems to be wreaking vengeance on those who oppose him. Indeed the play's most blood-chilling line is spoken by Joad when Athalie is about to make her last and fatal entry into the Temple (V.3.1668):

Grand Dieu, voici ton heure, on t'amène ta proie.

Yahweh is here perceived as some kind of ferocious and blood-thirsty animal and Joad seems to be rejoicing, not at the ending of a reign of evil but at the imminent destruction of a fellow human being, however wicked and deserving of punishment she may be.

As we have seen, the events recounted by Racine's source, the book of Kings, are those of a particularly savage period of Jewish history. Yet the details of Joad's character and conduct are of Racine's own invention and there is at times, in his depiction of them, almost a revelling in bloodthirstiness which is reminiscent of his first play, La Thébaïde ou les frères ennemis (1664), the equally savage story of the rivalry for the throne of Thebes which ended in the deaths of the twin sons of King Oedipus by his wife and mother Jocasta. One can only guess at the reasons behind Racine's evident taste for such barbarities.

Whatever we may feel about some of Joad's attitudes, there is no doubting his integrity. Unlike Mathan, he is not out for material gain, but bravely risks death in carrying out his duties, and particularly by protecting Joas. It might be argued that he stands to gain power if Joas becomes king, yet, unlike Athalie, he seeks power not for its own sake or for his own ends but in order to serve Yahweh, in whom his trust is unwavering. He has often been accused of fanaticism, but never of faltering in what he perceives as virtue. This single-minded integrity is, by a kind of paradox, accompanied by an astuteness and an understanding of the weakness of human nature which enables him both to strengthen the flagging courage of his own people and to be aware of possible chinks in his opponent's armour, as in the case of the love for gold which leads Athalie to her last fatal entry into the Temple. One is reminded, at a very different level, of Chesterton's priest-detective, Father Brown, whose experience in the confessional has left him with a deep knowledge of the functioning of the criminal mind and an appreciation of the frailty of his fellow beings which he, like Joad, applies, but rather towards their redemption than towards their destruction.

In the world in which he lives, Joad's single-mindedness is necessary. He leads a people whose past glories have given way to schism and dissension but which had been singled out by God to have special privileges, and also special responsibilities, towards God and man. Previous high priests and prophets had had to cope with monarchs who were unfaithful to their religion, but Athalie is militantly hostile to it. Since their religion was at the very root of the existence of the Jews as a people and since Athalie threatened Joas, the last hope for the Messiah who was to come and save them, it is small wonder that Joad is hard, austere and determined, responsible as he is for the survival and future salvation of his people and their religion. Moreover this hardness is reinforced by his perception of God, which, like that of many seventeenth-century

Christians, and especially Jansenists, was above all that of a severe judge who is ever ready to punish the wrongdoer.

Wrongdoers, for Joad, are those who culpably fail to acknowledge God and His Law, and consequently fail also to respect the rights of their fellow human beings. As we have seen, Joad attributes the killing of Naboth and the seizure of his vineyard by Athalie's mother, Jezabel, to her rejection of God. Athalie is just as bad, 'une impie étrangère', guilty of 'coupable insolence' (I.2.167) in rejecting Yahweh and His Law. Mathan is even worse: he is a renegade who has renounced Yahweh for personal advancement, as he himself admits (III.3.919 et seq.).

Joad is by any standards a harsh and uncompromising figure. He sees it his duty to denounce the wicked and to be ruthless in executing the divine judgement when called upon to do so. If such attitudes seem intolerant to a modern audience it should be recalled that Racine here is only being faithful to his source; indeed elsewhere in Kings, when Ahab failed to execute the Syrian king Ben-Hadad, whom he had defeated in battle, he was threatened with dire punishment by Yahweh for failing to carry out the divine will. Joad, then, is no harsher than the God portrayed by the writer of the Book of Kings. Moreover Racine himself wrote *Athalie* a mere half dozen years after Louis XIV, urged on by Mme de Maintenon, had agreed to the Revocation of the Edict of Nantes, which inaugurated a massive persecution of French Protestants. The theory of religious and ideological toleration in Europe was still hardly in its beginnings; its practice has varied greatly both before and since, and often for the worse.

As a general, Joad is astute, adaptable and ready and able to overcome a superior enemy by using his wits. It is he, not the professional soldier Abner, who defeats Athalie, realising that at the decisive moment his few untrained but committed Levites would be more reliable than all of Athalie's mercenaries. His first plan is a desperate one (IV.3.1345–61): the Levites, once Joas is crowned, are to sally forth and attack Athalie in her palace. This is forestalled, however, by the news that Athalie has surrounded the Temple and arrested Abner (IV.5.1422–30). Joad has thus lost his principal advantage, the element of surprise: already vastly outnumbered, without properly trained troops (although the Levites, used to butchering large sacrificial animals, were potentially tough opponents and unlikely to faint at the sight of blood), he is now thrown on to the defensive.

At this point he has recourse to his famous 'trick', which has sometimes been attacked as unscrupulous. Athalie, coveting David's 'treasure', which she presumes is of gold, enters the Temple and is trapped, the argument goes, by unfair means. But what are the realities of the situation? Politically, Athalie is usurping the throne. Militarily, she is a general besieging the Temple. The opposing general, Joad, the defender of Joas, the legitimate heir whom Athalie had tried to murder as a baby, is awaiting the almost inevitably successful assault on the Temple and the equally inevitable murder of the child Joas, once his identity is discovered, and of himself and his own family. In addition to these personal factors, the consequences of defeat for the future of the Jewish people are unthinkable. The hope of a Messiah of the House of David would finally disappear and with it the New Jerusalem, the future Christian Church, foreseen in Joad's prophecy (III.7.1159). So Athalie's willingness to enter the Temple poorly escorted — a gross error of tactical judgement on the part of any general — is, for Joad, literally a godsend, a clear answer to his prayer (I.2.292–93) and the only way out of an impossible military situation.

Dramatically, too, Athalie's move avoids the accusation of *invraisemblance* that a direct victory against such odds might have provoked. The play is not a miracle play; its plot is worked out by natural means through the passions of its characters. God intervenes not as a dramatically unacceptable *deus ex machina* but by allowing Joad to take advantage of Athalie's lust for gold. Interestingly, in the book of Kings Athalie enters the Temple only on hearing the applause for the newly-crowned king. There is no mention of her troops, her planned assault on the Temple or her negotiated entry. These are all of Racine's own invention and considerably heighten the drama.

Those who declare, like Mercanton (*32*, p.78), that 'la ruse de Joad est odieuse', are hardly fair or realistic, for they do not consider the alternative, which, as we have seen, is the destruction of Joas and the desecration of the Temple. As Sartre's *Les Mains sales* points out, it is difficult when in high office to keep one's hands clean of blood, and in that sense Joad is no exception, all the more so since he is involved in a virtual war. His 'trick', moreover, is not plotted in advance, but thought of on the spur of the moment and under extreme pressure. It is a *ruse de guerre* of the kind that has won battles and medals for many another general. Mathan characterises Athalie as being one who '...d'abord accablait ses ennemis surpris' (III.3.873). Failure to use every possible ruse against such an enemy as her would have brought any general disgrace and reprimand.

Racine himself, in some *Remarques sur Athalie* which he wrote while he was composing the play (*3*, p.951; *4*, V, p.205), defends what he called 'l'équivoque de Joad'. He compares it to Jesus's words 'destroy this temple' (John 2.19), by which he was referring to his forthcoming crucifixion, whereas his audience thought he was speaking of the Temple building. He also quotes St Ambrose's account of the martyrdom of St Lawrence. Lawrence was ordered by his judge to produce the riches of the Church, so he brought the judge some poor people who, for him, were real treasures in the eyes of God. The judge promptly ordered his execution.

Clearly there are innocent and less innocent equivocations, and circumstances change our attitudes to them. Racine may have felt somewhat sensitive in this regard since the Jansenists and their friends (notably Pascal in his *Lettres provinciales*) had previously attacked the Jesuits over their use of equivocation. Racine thought that Joad's use of it was legitimate, and, if one follows one's head, this view seems to me to be true. None the less the fact that Joad defeats his adversary in this way does perhaps lose him some sympathy and win some sympathy (undeserved but dramatically necessary) for Athalie.

Joad's wisdom and knowledge of human nature have already been mentioned, yet he often lacks the sympathy for his fellow human beings which frequently goes with such knowledge. He constantly and admirably trusts in God, but his verdict on his own people is to call them a 'peuple lâche et né pour l'esclavage' rather than to say, with St Augustine, 'there but for the grace of God go I'. His inner strength is admirable, but it verges on self-righteousness, while the failure, which we have noted, to take sympathetic account of the weakness of others is perhaps Joad's least likeable characteristic, all the more so since he is always proved to be maddeningly right. This strength of character is indeed a rare trait in Racine's theatre, if we see weakness and indecisiveness as being typically Racinian. Agrippine in *Britannicus* has strength, but she fails in her aims; Andromaque, in the play that bears her name, also has strength, but of a quieter, more unselfish kind. She also, unusually for a Racinian character, gets what she hopes for, although mainly through other people's failures. Seen in that context Joad has perhaps more in common with some of Corneille's heroes — Rodrigue, Auguste, Polyeucte — for, like them, he succeeds in attaining his objectives and, although he would not admit it, he does so seemingly by his own efforts, albeit divinely assisted.

He has, of course, more human traits. He shows true warmth and love towards Joas, particularly at the moment (IV.4) when he realises that in gaining a king he is losing a dear child, and his relationship with his wife Josabet, despite his frequent upbraidings for her failure to trust in God, is a loving and sometimes a touching one. His last words in the play speak of God as being '[pour] l'orphelin un père' but life gives him little opportunity to show the softer side of his nature. Like Churchill in 1940 he lives in times when all he can promise his people is blood, toil, tears and sweat until the enemy is defeated. In addition to this his theological intransigence makes him still more forbidding. Perhaps some aspects of his character may be illuminated by a comparison with the best of the clergy of a former age in countries like Ireland or Greece, trying to improve the lot of their flock in a harsh economic

and political climate whilst making them firmly toe the line as
regards faith and morals and encouraging them to preserve a sense
of national identity and culture.

What characterises Joad above all is his grandeur. The
breadth of his vision goes beyond the confines of his own times,
notably in the famous prophecy (III.7.1140–74), and is in keeping
with the epic tone which is one aspect of the play. He is an unusual
and austere figure, both in the context of the theatre and in that of
the world in general, but in spite of, or perhaps rather because of, a
personality which may be uncongenial to present-day tastes, the
character of Joad, like that of his arch-enemy Athalie, is a towering
and impressive one. They are worthy adversaries for each other.

5. Other Characters: Josabet, Abner, Mathan, Joas

Josabet

Josabet is one of the quietest characters in the play and her importance and value are thus not always fully appreciated. It is her past courage in saving the infant Joas from Athalie's knife which has allowed the action of the play, with its consequences for the Jewish people and the future foundation of Christianity, to happen in the first place. Moreover, courage is a daily requirement in her life. She is in constant danger from her stepmother Athalie, firstly because she is the daughter of Athalie's husband Joram by an earlier marriage, and therefore a possible claimant to the throne of Juda, and also, of course, because she is married to Athalie's arch-enemy, the high priest Joad. Yet, as has been noted, she is frequently upbraided by her husband for her lack of faith and courage, even though her record for courage is beyond reproach. Moreover the objections she makes to Joad's plans are mostly, if not always, reasonable ones, so he is sometimes unfair to her in this regard.

In a way she stands for ordinary sensible humanity finding itself in a situation in which a tougher-minded, more far-seeing leader sees that a sublime gamble, or act of faith, according to one's point of view, is the only real way out of the predicament he and his people are in, given that the day of reckoning can be postponed no longer. Josabet certainly finds it very hard in the seemingly impossible circumstances to imitate her husband's calm trust in the Almighty and to accept his cool assessment of the situation, particularly as regards the safety of Joas. In the event her emotions can and do cloud her judgement when the moment for real action arrives.

Her idea of smuggling Joas out of the Temple and taking him to Jehu (III.6) shows a certain political naïvety, since Jehu could not be relied on to protect the boy, but would be far more likely to use him as a bargaining counter in a sordid deal with Athalie: Joad's all-or-nothing gamble at least gives Joas a fighting chance of becoming king in his own right.

Josabet in fact gradually seems to lose hope as the action progresses (cf. IV.5.1433; V.4.1701) and her role becomes more passive as the play draws towards its end. Earlier on, however, she has two outstanding moments, one being the account of her brave rescue of Joas (I.2), the other (III.4) when she stands up to the insidious Mathan with great courage and dignity, as well as practical good sense, when he tries to interrogate her about the identity of the child. Dramatically, part at least of her role is to emphasise the degree of danger involved in the whole situation and to represent the loss of heart of even the best of her people in face of Athalie. Another is perhaps to show, by the warmth of her personality and by her unselfish love for Joas, that the cause of Yahweh has a human and positive face, in contrast with the harsh and denunciatory image usually (though not always) projected by her husband, to whom her loyalty and devotion is so total as to pass unnoticed. The fact that, as has been remarked earlier, he is always maddeningly right in his judgements makes one realise also that a prophet must at times be a very difficult man to be married to.

Successful marriages, incidentally, are few and far between in Racine's theatre. That of Josabet and Joad forms a singular exception to that rule, and their family is, equally unusually, a happy and united one, with their son, Zacharie, showing himself to be a very capable reporter of events off-stage (II.2, V.1), and courageous both in defying Mathan in the Temple (III.2) and in following his father's footsteps by the example he gives to the chorus when danger approaches (V.1). The sad irony is that such promise is doomed to future destruction at the hands of the one whom the family saved from death and helped to put on the throne.

Abner

Abner represents those pious and loyal Jews who want to see the tyrannical Athalie overthrown but who have despaired of ever seeing it happen. He, like them, thinks that the line of David is extinct, and his reactions no doubt reflect theirs. Like that other professional soldier, Burrhus, in Racine's *Britannicus*, he is honest but naïve: one example of this is his reminder to Joad, in a fine and memorable line (I.1.26), of a danger of which the High Priest must be only too aware: 'Pensez-vous être saint et juste impunément?' It is because of this naïvety that Joad tests Abner out very carefully, as we noted in discussing the plot. Joad cannot be sure whether or not a mistaken sense of honesty might ultimately make him remain loyal to Athalie rather than to the new legitimate king when the moment comes to reveal Joas's true identity. The declaration of allegiance which Joad obtains from Abner, 'De quelle ardeur j'irais reconnaître mon roi!' (I.1.146), is thus vitally important, although it does not guarantee prudent behaviour on his part.

In the light of this latter fact, what Joad does not say to Abner is in some ways as significant as what he does say, and this will clearly show in the actors' interpretations of the two parts. The High Priest is very careful not to take Abner too far into his confidence: he does not, for instance, tell him of his plans to overthrow Athalie. He adopts this policy for obvious security reasons — what a man does not know he cannot tell — and perhaps also in order to avoid any possible conflict of loyalties for Abner. As a result, when the moment of truth arrives and Athalie accuses Abner of leading her into a trap (V.5.1739), her general can honestly cry 'Reine, Dieu m'est témoin...' (V.5.1739).

Abner clearly owes both his survival through all the troubles and his position under Athalie to this honest simplicity. Even though, as Joad points out (I.1.79–82), he had served under King Joram and held the country together when Jehu had killed Joram's successor Ochosias, Athalie would surely have had him killed had she considered him to constitute a threat to her, as the news of his arrest (IV.5.1430) and imprisonment (V.2.1569) suggests. His honest presence must, however, have lent respectability to her régime. Abner thus served her purposes. But why did he remain in his post? Joad describes him as '...l'un des soutiens de ce tremblant Etat' (I.1.77). Indeed Abner's position must have allowed him to save his oppressed people from even worse troubles. This fact, together with his sense of loyalty and his naïvety, perhaps explains the otherwise puzzling fact that he was willing to continue in Athalie's service.

In the end, however, the professional soldier and man of action paradoxically finds himself forced to be a man of inaction. Yet by a further paradox it is this inaction which saves the day for the Jewish cause and provides a vital link in the unfolding of Racine's drama. Instead of bravely dying in a last desperate attempt to save the Temple, which he clearly expected, and was willing, to do, Abner finds himself first imprisoned, then ordered to serve as escort to Athalie in the Temple. His simple honesty then enables him to play his vital, though ironic, part in the liberation of his people, when the Queen mistakenly thinks that his presence guarantees her safe conduct both into — and out of — the building, thus bringing about her defeat and the dénouement of the play. So by a strange quirk of fate, honesty, in the case of Abner, clearly turns out to be the best policy, not only for himself and his people but, in the Christian context of Racine's play, for the whole human race. The 'Oui' with which he opens the play has far-reaching consequences.

Mathan

The evil-hearted Mathan belongs in Racine's tragic theatre with Narcisse, Néron's ill angel in *Britannicus* and, to a much lesser degree, with the cynical but somewhat less sinister Acomat in *Bajazet*. At a much greater remove one might even add Œnone in *Phèdre* to this band of characters who, for varying motives, give bad advice to those in power. The motives of the first two, however, are positively evil, whereas the second two act more out of weakness:

Acomat is trying to survive in a world of fellow predators and his selfishness is so gross that it could have verged on the comical in the hands of a lesser dramatist, whilst Œnone is trying, in her own incompetent way, to serve her mistress. Mathan and Narcisse, in contrast, are sinister, perfidious and hypocritical. The latter brings about the death of the young and innocent Britannicus, the former gives up Judaism so as to advance his career by becoming the high priest of 'une vaine idole', a deity in whom he does not even believe (III.3.919–22), thereby losing the right to any respect on the part of others, save, paradoxically, from Athalie herself.

We would expect Athalie, worldly as she is, to be particularly suspicious of the unscrupulous Mathan. Yet she treats him almost as a father confessor, notably in II.5, where she recounts her famous *songe* to him. Perhaps she really is taken in by him; certainly he is, by his own estimation, an expert at getting his way by flattering monarchs (III.3.932–44):

> J'étudiai leur cœur, je flattai leurs caprices,
> Je leur semai de fleurs le bord des précipices.

The danger for kings of listening to flatterers was, incidentally, a common theme in seventeenth century literature. Whether Racine had a particular axe, Jansenist or other, to grind by including these lines in *Athalie* is another question.

It is possible, as regards the relationship between Mathan and Athalie, that since neither appears to have any other friends, they both realise that they have only each other to rely on, in so far as either is reliable. Of the two, Mathan is more cynical about her than she is about him. Although he professes admiration for Athalie's 'grande âme' to Nabal (III.3.875), he is highly patronising about her to the latter behind her back and this only adds to our detestation of him: 'Elle flotte, elle hésite; en un mot, elle est femme' (III.3.876). Even readers in more sexist times could be scandalised by his tone of self-opinionated arrogance. On the theatrical level, however, the relationship between Mathan and the Queen offers great scope for interpretation to the actor and actress concerned.

Mathan's words and actions exemplify the worst excesses of the disciples of *raison d'Etat* whose ideas had outraged many people earlier in the century. They preached the idea that otherwise immoral actions could be justified if the State were in jeopardy, but Mathan counsels evil not just as an extreme course of action in the interests of the State, but routinely and almost as a reflex: Eliacin stabbed Athalie in her dream? — then kill him: 'On le craint, tout est examiné' (II.5.562). His main, indeed his only motivation, comes from self-interest; as he tells Nabal (III.3), he abandoned the Jewish God for Baal merely for personal advancement. He also seems to have done so in bad faith, confirming Joad's verdict on him as an 'infâme déserteur' (I.1.37), for the memory of Yahweh 'Jette encore en [son] âme un reste de terreur' (III.3.957) and his plan to destroy the Temple is intended to 'perdre tous [ses] remords' (III.3.962) by proving himself stronger than Yahweh.

Selfish, hypocritical, arrogant and bloodthirsty, Mathan is, then, a most detestable person. Joad's terrifying denunciation of him (III.5) wins the support of the whole audience. We can feel some kind of sympathy for Athalie since, despite her evil deeds, she has at least some dignity: her acts are, on the whole, open and public, however bad they may be. Mathan, on the other hand, is fundamentally underhand and mean-spirited. His sole aim, as we have seen, is to further his own narrowly selfish interests by manipulating others, and he has no respect for the lives of fellow human beings, admitting himself that he was 'prodigue surtout du sang des misérables' (III.3.944), as he had earlier demonstrated by urging Athalie to kill Joas.

Such totally evil characters, lacking any attractive features, are a real test of a dramatist's ability. They can easily turn out to be crude cardboard villains. Mathan, however, is both subtly drawn and highly convincing. For example, his sinister interrogation of Josabet (III.4) about the identity of Eliacin/Joas is a masterly portrait of insidiousness. It is also a masterly example of dramatic suspense and is followed by the equally dramatic turning of the tables brought about by Joad's denunciation of him (III.5). This, as we have noted in discussing the plot, foreshadows the final outcome of the play. Far from being a cardboard villain, then, Mathan is a memorable, indeed an archetypal one who makes an important contribution to the drama.

Joas

Child parts are much rarer in the French classical theatre than in Shakespeare, no doubt for practical reasons. Argan's small daughter, Louison, actually appears on stage in one scene of Molière's *Le Malade imaginaire*, but in Racine's *Andromaque*, although the heroine's son Astyanax is at the centre of the action, we never see him. In *Athalie* Racine was breaking new ground. In a sense, all of the parts in the first production were child parts, even though the children were playing adults, so perhaps Racine's young actresses did not need to have the fear of being upstaged which traditionally accompanies adults acting with children and animals. The part of Joas, however, represents a young child, nine or ten years old, and is really a very unusual one for the time.

It is the shortest part in the play, but not the least interesting. We see Joas first in a situation which is potentially very intimidating, facing Athalie's searching questions in a scene (II.7) whose dramatic impact is heightened for the audience by the knowledge that, unbeknown to both, she is the grandmother who stabbed him and left him for dead as a baby. From half-line factual replies his answers gain in confidence till he defies and ultimately silences the Queen with his crushing '...Pour quelle mère!' (II.700). As we have noted, Athalie dismisses this as the result of conditioning, but it is perhaps rather an example of the kind of presence of mind with which young children are wont to amaze their elders and thus a tribute to Racine's powers of observation. Certainly the confrontation is dramatically riveting.

Despite his brave stand against Athalie, Joas does not seem to be a precocious child and he gives an impression of genuine simplicity and sincerity, both here and in the scenes preceding his coronation off-stage. Yet his part is dominated above all by the dramatic irony which hangs over his future. This irony reaches its climax at the end of the play as he takes in the import of the curse which his grandmother hurls at him as she is dragged off to execution — an appalling experience for any child to undergo — and prays that it may not come true. The audience, however, knows that his prayer will not be answered — indeed, Josabet has already expressed her fears for him, given his ancestry (I.2.235–38).

His tragedy, then, will come, for blood will out. Inevitably, he will go the way of his grandparents, disobey Yahweh and come to a bad end. Worse, he will kill his childhood friend Zacharie, the son of the couple who saved his life and put him on the throne. Joas, of course, does not know this, but his fear is almost palpable. One wonders what orphan childhood traumas (lesser ones, clearly, but equally vivid) may have given Racine such an understanding of Joas and of his fears for the future. A clue, perhaps, lies in the kind of Jansenist teaching on the total corruption of human nature, even that of little children, which he must have received at Port-Royal and which has left its mark on young and sensitive souls even in more recent times. As François Mauriac wrote in his *Vie de Racine* (*31*),

> Le Jansénisme qui enlève tout à l'homme pour ne diminuer en rien la puissance de l'être infini, et qui accoutume un jeune être à vivre dans le tremblement, a laissé plus de trace qu'on n'imagine, au fond de nos provinces. (p.10)

6. Setting

The location of *Athalie*, in the Temple, is unique for a classical play. This confined setting is, of course, dictated by the Bible, but a confined setting is never confining for Racine: in memorable *récits* he takes us out in time and space to witness the death of Jezabel, Athalie's murder of her grandchildren, her arch enemy Jehu skulking in Samaria and the flight of her troops after Joas's coronation. Yet the setting is confining in another sense, since the narrow limits of the Temple make us feel first the claustrophobia of Joad and his followers, mentally and physically besieged, and later the claustrophobia of Athalie, caught like a rat in a trap and led out only to be butchered.

All this, of course, is typical of Racine, for his is a theatre of claustrophobia, of people caught, because of circumstances and their own natures, in situations from which there is no escape. He starts his plays at the moment when a difficult situation is about to turn into a predictably impossible one: the catalyst is introduced into the chemical mixture or, to borrow an image from Professor van Emden, the detonator is triggered. The consequent explosion is then all the more devastating because it takes place in a confined space, literally or figuratively. Indeed Racine's characters are often trapped physically as well as emotionally: the harem in *Bajazet*, Nero's court in *Britannicus*, the inner room from which Phèdre emerges, together with the labyrinth that lurks in her memory, all spring to mind. The feelings thus produced stem partly from the classical unity of place, the conventional interpretation of which had narrowed during the century from, perhaps, a whole town to one building — the so-called *palais à volonté* — or even a single room. Scenery as such was unimportant and needed only to be minimal, for the real setting was a place in the mind, the ultimate seat of the claustrophobe's fears.

Yet *Athalie* abounds in physical detail in comparison with other classical plays — no doubt because of the unique opportunities Racine was given, or had imposed on him, by the plot, the setting and the circumstances of his commission, and by the resources available at St-Cyr. Whether through choice or necessity, he was given unique opportunities with *Athalie* and he took them. With his large cast of *pensionnaires*, for instance, he was able to portray the Temple, the centre of God's presence for the Jews, and the busy life of its many inhabitants, with the chorus processing on and off stage and the Levites emerging from the wings at the climax. *Athalie*, like *Esther*, had clearly been intended to be full of movement and colour. Racine also adds further 'local colour' by references to Temple ceremonies (e.g. the purification of the marble floor which Athalie has profaned by walking on it, II.8.750).

Yet all this local colour is not there merely for its own sake. The physical setting of the Temple is linked to the action and to the day on which, as already noted, Racine makes it take place, the feast of Pentecost. This, as he points out in the preface to his play, is the feast of the Jewish Law, the Law which Athalie had so often flouted. Moreover the Temple was reputedly built on the spot where God had tested Abraham's trust in Him by asking him to offer his son Isaac in sacrifice, a test which God quickly ended once Abraham had proved his willingness to put obedience to Him above everything else. In fact Joad reminds Josabet, and with her the rest of his fearful people, of this when they learn that the Temple is surrounded (IV.5.1438). So both the Temple setting and the feast of Pentecost proclaim the contrast between the spirit of order, justice and obedience to the Law which they represent and the arbitrariness of Athalie's usurping rule.

To all this, of course, must be added the magnificent music — overture, choruses and *symphonie* to accompany Joad's prophecy — provided by Moreau, which amplifies the grandeur of the setting and underlines the beauty of Racine's verse. The music, as has been said, is often omitted, since most theatre companies do not have at their disposal anything like the resources which Racine had at St-Cyr for *Esther* and hoped to have for *Athalie*, but any production is the poorer without the music, if adequately performed. Certainly, though, there is no excuse whatever for omitting the choruses completely, as is sometimes done, for they can at least be spoken and their omission changes the spirit of the play totally, leaving out many, if not most, of the references to Yahweh as being a God of love rather than one of punishment. In a sense, indeed, the choruses are as much a commentary on Joad's values as they are on Athalie's. Moreover, to omit them is also to omit the links which make the action of *Athalie* a continuous one, without pauses between acts, a fact which Mercanton (*32*, p.78) points to as being symbolic: 'La démarche humaine a des arrêts; l'action divine ne connaît point d'intervalles.'

It is interesting to note that the maximum length of an act in most French seventeenth-century plays written for the professional stage was about twenty-five minutes; an interval was necessary so that the wicks of the candles that provided the stage lighting could be trimmed to prevent them from smoking. Perhaps the physical arrangements at St-Cyr were such as to make this unnecessary — a procession could easily include candle-snuffers/bearers or perform-ances could take place in daylight.

As we have seen, the setting of *Athalie* contains much preci-sion of detail and local colour, with its Temple ritual, its Levites and choruses and its transformation scene where the curtain is drawn aside to reveal Joas, crowned on his throne, to the astonished Queen. Yet it must be emphasised once more that the real action of the play, the real source of interest, lies in the minds and hearts of the characters: what we see on stage, magnificent as it can be, is but an outward manifestation of that. The action does not depend on the setting. Yet the setting does have a particular symbolic value, both for the Old and the New Testaments: Jesus, the future Messiah whose coming the action of the play makes possible, was later, when teaching in the Temple, to compare His death and resurrection to the destruction and rebuilding of the Temple, as was noted earlier in discussing Joad's *équivoque*.

The Temple, then, with all the symbolism and overtones of its site, its role as the centre of the Jewish religion, with its Holy of

Holies, the dwelling place of God Himself, makes a very particular contribution to the play, witnessing the downfall of the wicked but tragic Athalie and the restoration of the line of David, pointing to the future coming of the Messiah and underlining the affirmation, in the last line of the play, of the Law and its concern for the weak and needy as against the wicked and powerful.

7. Style and Poetry

It is hard to distinguish 'style' from 'poetry' in Racine, since each is a function of the other. As with classical architecture, the beauty of his plays lies not just in particularly 'poetic' speeches or passages, nor in extraneous decoration, but in the way in which, like a classical architect, but using words, he builds the structure of the whole poem (for his plays are dramatic poems), and in the way in which the various protagonists express their individual characters and their relationships with each other. In short, to describe the style is very often to describe the character, and vice-versa. This statement may sound obvious, but in a classical tragedy, where everything is reduced to bare essentials, it has a particular force. In Racine as for Buffon, but in a different sense, since it applies to the characters rather than to the author, 'Le style, c'est l'homme même': Joad declares his unswerving trust in God come what may; Joas, brave and innocent, defies Athalie; Josabet defends her young charge; Athalie shows her implacable and ultimately hopeless hatred for her divine adversary.

Thus the action of the play as we see it enacted on stage — the proclamation of their views, intentions and decisions by the characters and the resulting conflicts between them — is expressed ultimately through words (and, of course, accompanying gestures and movements) alone. What physical action there is springs from what the characters say to each other (e.g. Joad's crowning of Joas is a direct outcome of Athalie's threats). Indeed physical action in itself is much less interesting than the reactions and motives of the characters which lie behind it — the final physical battle for the Temple, for instance, in itself holds much less interest for the spectator than the process by which Athalie comes to enter it and what she says when brought to bay there. Moreover, the use of narration or description, *récit*, to convey physical action in the classical theatre is far more satisfying than the poor imitation which stage devices could provide.

Racine, for his production of *Athalie*, was relatively well off for acting space, but for the professional playwrights of his time acting room was very limited indeed and was reduced even more by the practice of allowing spectators actually to sit on the stage. Dramatists had to take account of these space limitations and this, together with the fact that violent action on stage was in any case forbidden by current literary theories, helps to account for the conveying of events by means of *récits*. With such small stages, moreover, the spectators were physically very close to the actors, and must have become involved at a correspondingly more intimate level, although acting styles tended to be somewhat declamatory. The *récit* was thus a normal part of theatre productions in Racine's time and today remains a powerful poetic and dramatic tool: as with radio as against television, having to use its imagination makes the audience participate far more actively in the drama.

The keynote of Racine's poetic style, in *Athalie* as elsewhere, could perhaps be called restrained grandeur. Since the subject matter is of high seriousness, the characters use elevated and carefully controlled language, showing the respect which they have for themselves and, normally, for each other. Departures from this norm usually serve to indicate anger or loss of self-control. Thus Joad excoriates Athalie's representative, Mathan (III.5), and later (V.5) even contemptuously addresses the Queen herself in the 'tu' form. This marked a scandalous mark of lack of respect towards a monarch in Louis XIV's day, but it also echoes the lack of respect for Joad's office which Athalie had shown and deliberately expressed in similar fashion. Such exceptions as these were shocking in the context of their time and emphasise the underlying violence. With Joad as with Athalie here it is not a question of loss of control (one cannot imagine him losing his self-control) but of his righteous anger at enemies of God whose evil behaviour has put them beyond the pale of respect.

Racine's normal style, however, is noble and elevated to befit its subject-matter. One illustration among many may be found in

I.1, where the contrast which Abner makes between the Pentecost ceremonies of former and present times serves to set the tone for the play. We notice his use of 'l'Eternel' for God (line 1), both a grander and a more respectful term; the formal yet precise use of adjectives: ('l'usage antique et solennel', line 2; 'la superbe Athalie/Dans un sombre chagrin', lines 51–52 — 'superbe' being used in the Latin sense of 'haughty'); the rivetingly brief character sketches: ('de Jézabel la fille sanguinaire', line 59).

Yet Abner's fine words pale beside the magnificence of Joad's first long speech, steeped in the language and spirit of the Bible. Many passages, from the Creation story onwards, are evoked and echoed by 'Celui qui met un frein à la fureur des flots' (line 61), where the repeated 'f' alliteration evokes the sound of the angry sea. Then Joad summarises his immutable faith in a wonderfully memorable line, which has the deceptive simplicity of true greatness: 'Je crains Dieu, cher Abner, et n'ai point d'autre crainte' (line 64). It conveys a tranquillity which comes from its content, an expression of Joad's total trust in God — note the difference in meaning between 'je crains Dieu', in the sense of 'awe', 'respect', and 'd'autre crainte' in the sense of 'panic fear' — and from the use of simple words, a matter which will be discussed a little later. The tranquillity is also conveyed by the combination of the vowels and consonants which make up those words (e.g. the sense of firmness of conviction conveyed by the repeated 'r' sounds and the 'defusing' of the threat conveyed in the sense of the word 'crainte' by the parallel use of the same nasal vowel which underlines the word 'point') and similarly by the steady rhythm of the four groups of three syllables, like calm and regular breathing, which make up this particular alexandrine.

Racine is the ultimate master of the alexandrine. None can rival the subtlety of his handling of it. He chooses words and puts them together so that they speak to us both by their sense and by what they convey through sound and rhythmic pattern. This presents marvellous opportunities to the actor, as in Athalie's account of her dream (II.5). The second line, for instance (line 491), describes how 'Ma mère Jézabel devant moi s'est montrée'. The two initial 'm' sounds, incidentally one of the first sounds a baby makes, convey Athalie's deep feelings for her mother and also suggest her trembling lip as she begins to relive her terrifying experience. The child-for-mother feeling is continued by the later doubly repeated 'm' and this effect is underlined by the 'soft' consonants 'j', 'z' and 'l' and the stressed final open vowels of 'mère' and 'Jézabel', perhaps hinting at a child's cry of fear. None of these sounds in isolation would produce such effects: it is their combination, together with the rhythm (2+4+3+3 syllables), giving an almost hesitant effect, as of one who cannot, for emotion, quite get into the normal flow of speech, which achieves Racine's object.

A few lines further down, in line 496, 'Pour réparer des ans l'irréparable outrage', the multiple repetition of 'r', not necessarily a harsh sound in itself, seems to me here — admittedly a subjective reaction, but perhaps not too far-fetched given the word *outrage* and the underlying current of violence in the play — to suggest rage, like some wild beast, snarling as it tears at its victim, as the dogs in fact were to do to Jezabel's corpse. The rhythm (4+2+4+2), together with the hesitation produced by the inversion of 'des ans...' could also suggest this. Yet the sense of the line is an elegantly emphatic, not to say *précieux*, way of explaining why Jezabel used makeup (and a reminder that for an audience which does not share Athalie's viewpoint Jezabel's very name conjures up the idea of a painted hussy, if not worse).

The *songe* is something of a set-piece speech, but this is unusual for Racine. Indeed, it is one of the few examples of his poetry to lend itself to inclusion in anthologies. As has been said, his poetry is dramatic poetry, and its function lies mainly in the general expression of the drama. Yet he could produce magnificent and memorable single lines, or even half-lines, which define a character or express an attitude in aphoristic form. We have already seen examples from the first scene of the play. Others have been quoted already: Mathan's advice to Athalie to have Joas killed on mere suspicion: 'On le craint, tout est examiné' (II.5.562) and Joas's devastating reply, already mentioned more than once, to

Athalie's invitation to live with her: 'Quel père/Je quitterais! Et pour...quelle mère!' (II.7.700).

The subject of *Athalie* is a religious one, but religious poetry is a notoriously difficult genre. When trying to express our deepest feelings we are most in danger of banality, mawkish sentimentality and sickly floweriness, and this is particularly true when we try to express our feelings about God. The problem was exacerbated for seventeenth-century writers by the fact that language had to be *bienséant*, suitably grand for the occasion. Although many of them tried to do so, few could master a style grand enough for addressing the Almighty; hence the number of awful prayer books of which the everyday speech of Molière's villain Tartuffe, for instance, is such an evident reflection.

Racine, however, was fully up to the task, as the choruses of *Athalie* show. Like the ancient Greek chorus, Racine's is a dramatic device, commenting on, and involving the audience in, the action, but its commentary is specifically religious and is often lyrical in tone, quite different from the spirit of most of the rest of the play by the way it sings of the love of God for man. The verse is of great beauty, as in this example (I.4.366–70):

> L'es*cla*ve *craint* le ty*ran* qui l'ou*trage*;
> Mais des en*fants* l'a*mour* est le par*tage*.
> Vous vou*lez* que ce *Dieu* vous *comble* de bien*faits*,
> Et ne l'ai*mer* ja*mais*?

The theme is from St Paul's Epistles (Romans 8; Galatians 4): we are not the slaves of some tyrannical deity, but the children of the one caring God who loves us as a Father and asks only to be loved in return, a clearly suitable theme for the orphans of St-Cyr.

Now the rhythm of French verse is the rhythm of ordinary French speech, and it divides itself into groups of sounds by stressing the last sounded syllable of each of the most important words, marked in italics in our example. There are no fixed stress-patterns as there are in English verse (thus, for example, limericks are not really possible in French without gross distortion of the proper stress rhythms). So in the first line of our quotation the importance of the words 'esclave', 'craint', 'tyran' and 'outrage' is naturally emphasised by the voice. More, the effect created by the rhythm thus produced becomes correspondingly more emphatic and menacing because of the meaning of those words. In the next line, however: 'Mais des en*fants*...' the voice (like the children it speaks of) feels free to run — in this case, straight to the fourth syllable, then to the other important words that the rhythm emphasises — 'amour' and 'partage'.

After these two ten-syllable lines the pace changes with an alexandrine. We notice the stressed verbs, notably 'vou*lez*' — one can only love from free choice — and '*com*ble' — God is not mean with His gifts. Finally comes the six-syllable line with its renewed emphasis on the importance of love and the challenge of the final word — never? — and the implied answer — impossible.

The choruses are a rather special example of Racine's ability as a religious poet, but virtually the whole play is a faithful reflection not only of the incidents described in his immediate biblical sources but also of the religious spirit and language of the Bible as a whole. In this, as has already been mentioned, he is following in the footsteps of his sixteenth-century predecessor, Garnier. Any decent critical edition of *Athalie* will be full of footnotes giving references not only to Kings but to the Psalms (many of which Racine himself had previously translated) and to many other books of the Bible. Indeed the whole play is steeped in the poetry of the Bible, which, although France lacks an equivalent having the linguistic beauty and influence of the English Authorised Version (the Latin Vulgate being perhaps its equivalent in Catholic countries), is one of the foundation stones of French, as it is of British, culture.

Joad's famous prophecy (III.7) is a particularly good example of the way in which the Bible is part and parcel of Racine's poetic personality in *Athalie*. The first of its two sections draws on both Old and New Testaments, notably the foretelling by Jesus of the destruction of the Temple (e.g. Matthew 23,24), but Racine blends his sources very cleverly and adds to them in the spirit of the original so that it is hard to tell which is Racine and which the Bible.

The second section is based mainly on St John's Apocalypse (the book of Revelation) foretelling the New Jerusalem of the Christian Church which the Messiah was to establish. Once again, however, Racine blends in, and embroiders on, other Old and New Testament texts.

Racine's poetic style was earlier characterised as being one of restrained grandeur, but this grandeur is never allowed to degenerate into mere verbosity and grandiloquence. Indeed Racine, like Shakespeare, resorts, for some of his greatest effects, to utter simplicity, as do people in real life who suddenly come to realise and accept, at moments of great stress, what has happened to them. So King Lear, carrying the body of his daughter Cordelia, at last understands that all life has gone from it and utters the heart-rending monosyllables, 'She's dead as earth'. Such moments of recognition were, for Aristotle, the soul of tragedy and, far from detracting from the tragic grandeur, the simplicity of the language here enhances it.

Like Lear, Athalie also uses simple words, though very different in tone and spirit, in her last scene, when she spits out the famous 'Dieu des Juifs, tu l'emportes' (the Chorus addresses God as *tu*, but one senses here the same kind of contempt as in Joad's use of *tu* to her). These words express both her own deep-seated anger, hatred and agony and also the tragic significance of the moment. At this supreme point in the play, she recognises that the overweening pride that made her pit her strength against God, not just the Gods, has brought about her inevitable downfall. She acknowledges her defeat both to herself and to the audience and, as we have seen, despite her wickedness, even gains sympathy for her plight.

Racine was a true master of his craft. One small example of this fact is to be found in Zacharie's description of himself serving in the Temple with 'le jeune Eliacin', who, like him, was dressed in a 'long habit de lin'. The word 'lin' could well have been put in by a lesser poet simply to provide a rhyme, but in fact the linen robe was characteristic of the Levites who served in the Temple, so the word adds an element of local colour and authenticity to the description and gives Racine his rhyme in the process.

Images are often a significant feature of Racine's theatre — the contrast between light and darkness in *Phèdre*, for instance, symbolising, among other things, the heroine's perception of good and evil and her descent from the sun-god. In *Athalie* the word whose recurrence is most striking is 'sang', sometimes used in the sense of 'lineage' (a theme discussed elsewhere), occasionally also in literal references to Temple sacrifices, but most often in the context of slaughtering human beings. Carnivorous animals are also frequently mentioned, either figuratively, like the wolves from which Joas says he was rescued (II.7.642), or literally, like the dogs which devoured Jezabel and with which Joad threatens Mathan (III.5.1038), and in the same scene the word 'proie' is used by Joad to Mathan (line 1040) as well as in his famous line addressed to God (line 1668).

As in *Phèdre*, darkness is evoked: 'ténébreux', 'noir', 'noirceur', (I.1), but there is little mention of light, save in Joad's prophecy (III.7) and the following chorus. Poison and corruption are also mentioned, mostly by Josabet and Joad: 'empestée', 'poison', (III.4.1016–17); 'infecter', (III.5.1026). The most positive images refer to plants and their growth, and, as might be expected, occur mostly in the choruses: 'fleurs', 'fruits', (I.4.323–24); 'lis', (II.9.781), but flowers can also strew a primrose path (II.9.821) or can be untimely cut (IV.6.1491–93) and a tree can dry up (I.1.140) and its fruit be torn off unripe or nipped in the bud (I.2.285–86) — here it is Joad who is talking of his wishes for Joas should the latter ever betray his faith. Altogether the pattern of recurring images is a faithful reflection of the sombre and bloody character of much of the play.

8. Tragedy

The title of *Athalie* would suggest that it is the tragedy of Athalie. If we read what Racine says about his play in the preface, however, we find this:

> Elle a pour sujet Joas reconnu et mis sur le trône; et j'aurais dû dans les règles l'intituler *Joas*. Mais la plupart du monde n'en ayant entendu parler que sous le nom d'*Athalie*, je n'ai pas jugé à propos de la leur présenter sous un autre titre, puisque d'ailleurs Athalie y joue un personnage si considérable, et que c'est sa mort qui termine la pièce.

There is, then, a basic ambiguity about the play. Historically it is the story of Joas, but dramatically it is the story of Athalie. Its 'proper' subject is the triumph of Joas and the restoration of the line of David, which was to lead to the coming of Jesus as Messiah, arguably an epic rather than a tragic subject, and, apparently at least, highly edifying for the young ladies of St-Cyr. Yet part and parcel of that subject is the story of Athalie, scarcely edifying, save perhaps as a negative example, but which clearly entitles the play to its designation as a tragedy. These two aspects are interdependent. Clearly it is Athalie who provides the dominant element, but we must not lose sight of the first one, which will be discussed later.

Turning to the second, tragedy is notoriously difficult to define, yet *Athalie* is universally recognised as a masterpiece of the genre. Where, then, does its tragedy lie? The traditional view of the tragic hero, emanating from Aristotle, is that of a person of middling virtue who because of pride undergoes a fall, thus moving the audience to pity and fear and inducing in them a process of *katharsis*, or purification of their passions. Yet, as has been noted many times, Athalie is far from being a person of middling virtue. As to her pride, an attitude whereby the hero behaves as superior to others, and frequently as equal or superior to a deity, this too will be examined later.

Since, given Athalie's wickedness, the Aristotelian theory appears to present some difficulties, it might be argued that it would be better to try another approach in order to characterise the nature of her tragedy. For instance, Racine himself, in the preface to *Bérénice*, speaks of 'cette tristesse majestueuse qui fait tout le plaisir de la tragédie'. He is here defending the idea that *Bérénice* is still a tragedy since, although its two lovers do not die, their desperate parting for ever is tragic enough. In *Athalie*, however, the scale of the emotions is far too great and too complex to seek its tragic nature in *tristesse*, even with the much stronger meaning which that word had in the seventeenth century.

Truth to tell, the tragic nature of *Athalie* does not easily fit into formulas, but the Aristotelian objection to the wicked heroine keeps returning: how can a multiple child murderer — and one can think of few worse crimes — be thought of as tragic rather than monstrous? Many critics, following Voltaire, have sought a solution to the problem by forgetting Athalie's criminal record and seeing her, in the punishment she receives from God via Joad, as almost more sinned against than sinning. Without going so far as that, Odette de Mourgues, for instance, in her excellent and lucid book, *Racine or the Triumph of Relevance (36*, p.121), holds that Athalie is unfairly treated, despite her crimes.

She argues the case in terms of the important distinction between moral order and tragic order. Moral order is the accepted code of conduct which normally prevails, against which the events of the play constitute a revolt and which is restored at the end of the play. The tragic order is a separate code whereby the hero or heroine is opposed by a superior force which inevitably crushes him or her. This force is unfair and amoral and has, indeed, nothing to do with the moral order. It is ultimately an aesthetic device used to highlight the predicament of the hero. Thus Phèdre's adulterous, if not incestuous, love for her stepson Hippolyte, which leads to his death, is against the moral order, which is duly restored at the end of the play, but in the tragic order her love is unjustly imposed on Phèdre by the goddess Venus as part of a vendetta against her family. Her fate is unfair and unmerited in the moral order, but in the tragic order it is the lot of the heroine, and its aesthetic result is to increase the pity and fear we experience on her behalf.

This would seem to be clearly true in the case of Phèdre, but can it be said to be true in the case of Athalie? Can we in fact separate the tragic order from the moral order in the case of a truly wicked hero or heroine? Aristotle's idea that the hero should be of middling virtue surely stems from the fact that the hero's moral status, whether it be high or low, largely determines our reaction to him. The extent of our sympathy will vary according to the character involved and to the circumstances, and Phèdre, virtually forced against her will by the curse of a goddess into a passion which she resists with all her might, attracts our understanding far more readily than does the totally selfish, vindictive, power-hungry grandchild-killer Athalie, whose misdeeds, I would argue, have certainly not been forced on her by Yahweh. She does not, in fact, see her actions as misdeeds and defends them vigorously, notably in II.5.

Athalie, of course, is not the only exception to Aristotle's prescription. Other wicked heroes and heroines have been portrayed by the greatest dramatists — Shakespeare, Corneille and indeed Racine himself — despite his strictures. Their wickedness, however, tends to be duly recognised and accepted, whereas the tendency of those critics who try to minimise Athalie's wickedness has not been as helpful in coming to a better understanding of her tragic nature as would a direct acceptance and confronting of it.

Let us therefore consider how Athalie's fall comes about. For de Mourgues, it is God's doing in the tragic order, but He is no *deus ex machina* and she is no mere puppet manipulated by His unseen hand. It is through her passions that He brings about her downfall, which comes as a fulfilment of Joad's prayer (I.2.293) that she should be filled with an 'esprit d'imprudence et d'erreur'. Indeed God works subtly in exploiting those passions. Moreover He exploits her better feelings as well, indeed just as much as He does her worse ones, and in doing so works 'in the unfair, cruel and amoral way in which fate always works in a tragedy'. At the end we are left with a feeling of 'wanton gratuitousness on the part of fate, since the ruler who replaces her will be morally worse than she is' and this is why we give her our sympathy (*36*, p.123). The amoral, unfair tragic order, then, destroys Athalie, but running in parallel with it and prevailing at the end of the play is the moral order, the Christian order, that of Racine's audience: 'whatever the evil ways of individual kings, the concept of the good Christian ruler remains an unshaken value and divine justice shines on ' (*36*, p.124).

Apart from the very doubtful contention that Joad was to become morally worse than Athalie, a point that the Bible at least does not appear to substantiate (see II Chronicles 24 for his later biography), two difficulties seem to me to be involved here. The first is that of Athalie's passions and what it is that brings about her downfall. It seems to me that it is her greed for gold, together with the desire to gain possession of Joas (perhaps out of pity and care for him, perhaps in order to have him under her control), which induces her to go to her doom in the Temple and that this comes as an answer to Joad's prayer.

I believe, however, that it does not happen as an effect produced by a cause. The question of how prayers are answered, whether it is by direct divine intervention to change the course of history or otherwise, is a fascinating one; it has, moreover, a particular relevance here in the context of the drama. Surely we are not to see God as stimulating the immoral passion of greed in Athalie? In fact, He did not need to, for, as Joad knows, it was there already, indulged by Athalie, as it had been by her mother Jezabel, who had had Naboth killed because she coveted his vineyard, and it was ever ready to show itself. Joad's prayer is therefore probably based less on the desire to have the Almighty do the devil's work than on a shrewd guess at the way in which Athalie might behave if her passions came in conflict with the need to make a rational judgement.

The second difficulty is that if we separate the moral from the tragic order in *Athalie*, the divinity lying behind and guaranteeing unshakeable values and divine justice in the play must also be the same God who leads Athalie into evil by exploiting her passions, and this seems to me to be inconsistent. Moreover, I am not sure that we can talk about the 'wanton gratuitousness of fate' operating in *Athalie* in the same way as it operates, say, in Greek tragedies, since the whole play is an explicitly religious play and written in terms of the Bible, and consequently, at least in principle, in terms of the idea that the universe is governed not by some blind and abstract Fate, but rather by some sort of Divine Providence.

This does not provide easy solutions to the play's problems; on the contrary, it perhaps makes them harder to solve. It also perhaps helps to account for the fact that seventeenth-century writers and artists preferred to portray pagan gods rather than the Christian God in their works (other than in specifically religious ones). The practice, incidentally, had been disputed around the middle of the century, notably by Desmarets de Saint-Sorlin, who argued that the pagan gods should be excluded from art and literature on the grounds that they were false and therefore *invraisemblables*. This dispute was to lead to a wider one on the superiority of modern writers over the Ancients, and on the idea of progress, which lasted into the eighteenth century.

To sum up my objections to de Mourgues's argument as I understand it: if God is unfair and amoral in his treatment of Athalie in the tragic order, using her passions to destroy her yet leaving the moral order intact, as happens in Racine's 'pagan' plays, then the guarantor of that moral order is the same God whose conduct she sees as being so unfair and amoral. I am not therefore convinced that to distinguish between the moral order and the tragic order is appropriate in the case of *Athalie*.

Certainly the God presented in the play is often rebarbative (e.g. his use of Jehu to massacre Athalie's family) and sometimes ambiguous, viewed by Joad as a harsh avenging judge and compared by him to a predator, yet perceived by the choruses as the loving father of His children, the human race. This ambiguity, however, is not confined to the play: it is to be found in the Bible. If the God of the play appears amoral, so sometimes does that of its sources, a fact which Biblical scholars nowadays tend to account for by anthropomorphism and by the historical conditions in which the writers of the different books lived and which coloured their perceptions: a writer living in harsh times would thus have a correspondingly harsh image of God, who has consequently not always had a fair press from His faithful followers. Far from playing down the harshness and moral ambiguity of Yahweh in the play, moreover, Racine sometimes increases it. It was he who added the idea of Athalie's feeling some trace of pity for Eliacin/Joas (II.7.654), a good instinct which plays at least some part in the fateful decision to enter the Temple which leads to her destruction.

I would argue, then, that the moral order of the play is that of the Bible as Racine perceived it. That order includes all the harshness of certain parts of the Old Testament but also, particularly but not only in the choruses, all the love for humanity that is expressed in many other parts of both the Old and the New Testaments. This moral order, I would further argue, is not too far removed from the play's tragic order. What, then, is the nature of the latter?

The whole problem, I believe, centres around the importance of the role to be attributed to Christianity and, more specifically, to Jansenism in *Athalie*, if not in Racine's theatre as a whole. This influence has sometimes been played down by critics, since it is impossible to prove conclusively what exactly was Racine's commitment to it at the various stages of his life. Certain extreme positions seem to me untenable in the matter. However, we must remember that Racine wrote *Athalie* at the request of the pious Mme de Maintenon and that it is not only a religious play but also a masterpiece of religious poetry. The balance of evidence would thus lead me to think that whatever the character of his earlier plays had been, Racine, in writing such a play, was unlikely to establish a tragic order for it which was clearly unfair and amoral.

I would see the tragic order of *Athalie* more as expressing the will of a God whose purposes and actions, however harsh they may appear to us, are totally beyond our understanding. Yet these purposes and actions must be accepted unquestioningly because they come from the source of all wisdom, who is also a God of love for those who are willing to accept Him. This view seems to me all the more likely since by the time he wrote *Athalie* Racine had returned to the assiduous practice of his religion, a fact which could be ascribed to mere outward conformism were it not for the sympathy he showed, at personal cost, for the unpopular cause of Jansenism and for the fact that his last wish was to be buried at Port-Royal at the feet of his old teacher, M. Hamon.

But let us return to Athalie's fate. Is it in fact an unfair one inflicted by an amoral deity? In the light of what has just been said, 'incomprehensible' would be a more appropriate term than 'amoral' to characterise the ultimate guarantor of morality in the play. It must not be forgotten, moreover, that His purposes and commands are expressed as much by the choruses as by the rest of the play, and particularly by the refrain of the chorus that ends the first act: He wants people to love Him and obey His law. Turning next to Athalie, she is certainly not, as we have seen, like Phèdre, struggling in vain against an urge which she believes to be wrong. She is not the weak, inoffensive victim of a goddess's vendetta; she is, as we have insisted, a fierce usurper. She may have been temporarily weakened, but she still actively pursues to the end a blood feud based on her own and her family's desire to rule as they see fit, however arbitrarily that may be. Indeed her final order is to kill the child king Joas as soon as she realises who he is (V.6.1729). She is certainly not a mere prey to her passions, either. If it is they which destroy her, she, unlike Phèdre, has done nothing to try and control them: on the contrary. Moreover, as has already been suggested, although her enemies, typified by Joad, may be harsh, their motives are not selfish like hers.

Her fate is ultimately, then, an unjust one: she proudly accepts full responsibility for her actions and her fate is surely no more an unfair one than that of her fellow usurper Lady Macbeth — indeed the audience would be very shocked if she should triumph and be allowed to kill Joas, Joad and Josabeth. Moreover, far from that fate being gratuitous, the long-term consequence of her well-deserved defeat, despite the later infidelity of Joas, is enormously positive: the renewed possibility of the coming of the Messiah.

The moral order and the tragic order in *Athalie* thus seem to me to be much closer than in the case of Racine's 'secular' plays. In the latter, the two orders may indeed be separate and the hero's fate may be arbitrary. The power Athalie challenges, however, is not a blind, arbitrary Fate, nor some wilful anthropomorphic deity that kills for sport, but the God whose Law she spurns by her selfish and arbitrary behaviour and whose servants succeed in defeating her against all the odds. It may be that Joad's prayer about 'un esprit d'erreur' is answered, in the sense that Athalie makes an error of judgement in going unescorted into the Temple, but she goes there of her own volition, impelled largely by her own greed for gold.

Yet if she is not unjustly treated, how, then, is Athalie tragic, given her past behaviour, her personality and the values she represents? She does not naturally inspire pity — the pity we feel instinctively tends to be rather for her victim, the child Joas and for his rescuer, Josabet — and the fear we feel in her regard is at times not so much the kind of fear at the fate of the tragic hero of which Aristotle speaks as sheer terror at the force of her personality and the potential for violence which we know it represents. And yet, as we saw when discussing her character in an earlier chapter, we do feel some sympathy and even a kind of admiration for her, and this is perhaps not unrelated to the pride which was mentioned earlier. It is against Yahweh, the God of the Jews, that her pride pits her — her challenge to Him to produce the Messiah now that the line of David is, as she thinks, extinct (II.7.734) is perhaps the supreme example of hubris. She is clearly no equal for Him; no mere human being can take on a god and win. Yet in her struggle she displays two great qualities of the Aristotelian hero: dignity and grandeur.

Perhaps, then, the spectacle of a human being, wicked though she may be, taking on not just a god but The Infinitely Superior Power and, inevitably, losing is what makes Athalie supremely tragic. Moreover, in her defeat she shows that she does not lack courage, and that is something which always commands admiration, however grudging, from reader or audience, as with Molière's

Dom Juan, Mozart's Don Giovanni and Milton's Satan: 'Better to rule in Hell then serve in Heaven' — not a very moral nor indeed a wise counsel, perhaps, but one that appeals to something in us all. Athalie defying the Almighty drags from us a certain respect which is detached from conventional moral values. We do not question those values, we do not think Athalie is being unfairly punished for spurning them, but we still respect her defiant spirit. Her command to Abner when she pulls herself together after the initial shock of finding herself surrounded: 'Laisse là ton Dieu, traître/Et venge-moi' (V.5.1739) is a notable example of this.

It was said earlier, when discussing Athalie's character, that this reaction is in some way reminiscent of Corneille's idea of *admiration*, whereby we are filled with wonderment at the person whose extraordinary deeds we witness, whether those deeds are virtuous or evil. This is not to suggest that such was Racine's intention: indeed he criticised Corneille for presenting deliberately exaggerated characters. Yet it is hard not to be struck with wonderment by Athalie. Whatever wickedness she has done or may do, she goes down fighting, verbally at least. She admits to having lost the battle: 'Dieu des Juifs, tu l'emportes', but, like Cléopâtre in Corneille's *Rodogune*, who, as already noted, clearly served as an inspiration for Racine's very much more subtly drawn character, she does not give in but goes to her death proclaiming that, in modern biological parlance (which accords remarkably closely with Racine's preoccupation with heredity), her genes are still alive in Joas and also accurately predicting that murder will out in due course.

This kind of respect for Athalie's courage is, of course, only part of the story, but it seems to me to be one of our reactions to her and one which does not always receive sufficient attention. More important, and on a deeper level, is the fact, once again previously noted, that the spectacle of a fellow human being, whatever evil she has done, suffering such a catastrophe cannot leave us unmoved without diminishing our own humanity. We are moved by the downfall of Athalie in spite of her wickedness. Moreover the moral ambiguity surrounding some of the circumstances of that fall does contribute to our reactions. She ignores Mathan's appalling advice in II.5.562, but if she had in fact had Eliacin/Joas killed, she would herself have survived. More particularly, the fact that Athalie's first glimmer of humanity in feeling some pity for young Joas ('Je serais sensible à la pitié?' II.7.654) is in some way linked with her downfall undoubtedly disturbs our sense of justice and inclines us to side with her as the underdog in an unequal struggle, even though her murderous reaction of recognising Joas brings quick disillusionment as to her real character.

How can the apparent injustice of a virtuous reaction leading to Athalie's downfall be accounted for? An explanation becomes possible if one accepts, as has been suggested above, the influence of Jansenism, and in particular of the Jansenist theology of grace, on Racine at the time of *Athalie*. Its spirit and influence on his plays are difficult to disentangle from that of the fatalism so characteristic of Greek drama, which he also came to know so intimately at Port-Royal. The Greeks, like the Jansenists, but for very different reasons, portrayed human beings as powerless to conquer their own passions and rule their own lives, even if they want to.

What I speak of as 'Jansenism', however, is a very complex phenomenon, and represents more the extreme end of a theological school extant in Racine's day, which took its inspiration from the writings of St Augustine on grace and which became the object of persecution. It is easy to misrepresent its ideas and I am conscious of over-simplifying them. There is a note on Jansenism in the form of an appendix at the end of this book. However, in practical terms, the Jansenist view was that human nature is so corrupt that no human being can do any action pleasing to God without a special grace, or act of help, from Him. Unaided human actions, even attempts at virtuous acts, are meaningless — they have no validity without the help of grace and God alone decides who is to receive that grace; all that human beings can do is wait and hope that it will be granted to them.

As far as Athalie was concerned, the author of that grace was her sworn enemy. In the Jansenist perspective He could, had He wanted, have given her His grace in spite of her attitude towards Him, but He chose not to. The reasons for this refusal were beyond human comprehension but, for the Jansenists, did not conflict with His nature as a loving God: that was taken for granted. So, viewed in that light, no action of Athalie's could do any good, and she was predestined to inevitable failure, as tragic a predicament as that of any Greek hero and certainly calculated to induce both pity and fear in the spectator, who may well, unlike Joad, feel impelled to say, with St Augustine, the great theological authority and virtual patron saint of the Jansenists, 'There but for the grace of God go I'.

The Jansenists were, like many other Christians, overwhelmed by the idea of God's almighty power and justice and of man's total unworthiness. However, they perhaps tipped the theological balance too far in one direction by minimising the role of Free Will, and it was, amongst other things, the consequences of this for our moral responsibility which led to their condemnation by the Church, whose viewpoint on the matter was rather more sympathetic to sinners. Many people find that, humanly speaking, the Jansenist theology of grace is repellent and frightening. Applied to a tragedy, however, as in *Athalie*, it makes magnificent theatre.

9. Significance

Athalie is both a political and a religious play. In it, the workings of power politics, the machinations of a game in which the winner takes all and there are no holds barred, are expertly observed: Mathan is willing to change his religion in order to become high priest of Baal when he realises that he cannot become high priest of Yahweh and to suggest killing Joas on the mere suspicion that he might pose a threat; Athalie has killed her grandchildren, the legitimate heirs, after the death of her son Ochosias, in order to seize the throne for herself and defy Yahweh; finally Joad succeeds in turning the tables on both Mathan and her, against all the odds, by exploiting her weakness for gold.

The religious drama, however, gives a new and broader dimension to the political one. Athalie sees matters largely in terms which are political and which, since she is an absolute monarch, are also personal. She therefore considers that she can do what she wants in what she holds to be her own kingdom. Also, as a follower of Baal, she will brook no interference from the Jewish God and His partisans who had been responsible for the death of her mother and her family. Yet Athalie's Jewish opponents have a very different perspective on the matter. They see themselves as God's Chosen People, persecuted by her for their beliefs. Their opposition to her is carried out in the name of decency and of justice, particularly for the weak and innocent, and they live in the hope of the eventual coming of the Messiah. For Racine's intended Christian audience the perspective was wider still, since for them the survival of the line of David and the coming of the Messiah in the person of Jesus were vital for their future and for that of all humanity, as Joad's prophecy makes clear. Both the political and the religious aspects of Racine's play are united by the fact that it is a tragedy.

The preface, as was noted earlier, tells us that *Athalie* is the story of both the restoration of Joas to the throne and of the downfall of the usurping queen. Since, ultimately, interpretations of *Athalie* tend to turn on the religious sympathies of the spectator or reader, one or other of these two aspects is liable to be emphasised accordingly. This seems to me to be understandable: it is tempting, for example, for the Christian believer to identify with a solution in which the future existence of his faith is threatened and, in taking sides, to see Joad, the champion of Joas, as completely virtuous and Athalie, his would-be assassin, as beyond all sympathy.

It is equally tempting for the non-believer to see Joad as a dangerous and intolerant fanatic. Yet too close a personal identification can distort, and it is easy to forget that *Athalie*, in the last analysis, is a work of art. Indeed in the past, interpretation of *Athalie* has been bedevilled in France by old politico-religious quarrels between clericals and anti-clericals. On the one hand the play has been seen as *littérature engagée*, often on behalf of the black-and-white triumphalist views of a certain kind of Catholicism, and on the other by a 'Voltairean' view of the play as an anti-clerical tract, with Joad, standing for the bogeyman of intolerant clericalism, playing the villain, and Athalie representing his unfortunate victim.

Yet past critics on both sides of that sad divide, now crossed by many bridges, have much to teach us, and the play does not have to be seen from one angle only. The more human face of the French Church since the war has changed the attitude of many people towards it and an understanding of the appalling religious intolerance of Voltaire's times has long since helped virtually all Catholics to understand why Voltaire took the view of the play which he did, even if his characterisation of Athalie herself may seem to them to be mistaken. Interpretations may still depend on the beliefs or sympathies of the spectator, but it is to be hoped that the old bitterness, at least, has largely, if not entirely, disappeared.

It is possible, then, for the Christian to sympathise, without ultimately agreeing, with a view of the play which sees Athalie as the victim of a fanatical conspiracy: Joad, harsh and frequently

barbaric in his views, is not the only one of his party to be so. Five
lines from the end of the play, for instance, a Levite says of Athalie
that Jerusalem 'Avec joie en son sang la regarde plongée'. One is
reminded, in one's horror, of the famous ironic line (I.5.280) from
Tartuffe: 'Les sentiments chrétiens, mon frère, que voilà!' Viewed
in a broader Christian perspective, it is also possible to see the play
as being about the eventual triumph of goodness. Despite all the
evil, both present and future, in the world — exemplified by the
misdeeds of Jezabel and Athalie, by the bloodthirstiness of Joad and
his companions and by the fact that Joas will turn out to be not
much better than his grandmother — evil will still not conquer in
the long run. When God Himself comes into the world in the person
of Jesus, He too will be betrayed and cruelly put to death, but His
resurrection will guarantee for all humanity the future coming of a
far better kingdom, which is not of this world.

   All this, it can be argued, is implicitly contained in Joad's
prophecy. It can similarly be argued that it may not necessarily
correspond in theological detail to Racine's Jansenist view of
Christianity. What is clearly explicit in the play, however, is the fact
that with the 'resurrection' of Joas (a possible prefiguration of that
of Jesus, incidentally) the restoration of the line of David will lead
to the birth of the Messiah and the coming of a new Jerusalem,
which Racine's note (III.7.1159) identifies with the Church, having
as its mission to serve the good of the human race by bringing it to
God. This religious element is so clearly central to the play that to
minimise its importance by seeing the play as merely or mainly
political, with overtones of religious fanaticism, and centred on a
power struggle in which Athalie loses to Joad, seems to me greatly
to reduce its stature and, in particular, its significance as a tragedy.

   The story of the fall of Athalie is not only tragic, but her
tragedy is on the grandest possible scale, since she, a human being,
pits herself against the greatest of all deities. She believes that by
destroying the line of David she has succeeded in frustrating His
plans for the future of mankind, as she makes clear in her challenge
to God, made in the Temple itself (II.7.734), to produce the
Messiah. In the light of this, if one is willing to effect at least a

willing suspension of disbelief in the coming of the Messiah and His kingdom, the tragedy of *Athalie* takes on an epic scale and aspect which enhances its status as a tragedy, and makes it, indeed, unique: Racine's subject is the ultimate tragic subject, that of a human being taking on the true God and, fortunately for the human race, losing.

It is not only the non-Christian, moreover, who may be called upon to suspend disbelief for aesthetic purposes. If the play is to be viewed in the Jansenist perspective which was suggested earlier, most Christian believers will also need to suspend their disbelief. They will, for the purposes of the play, have to accept that a supposedly loving God can refuse His love and help to a sinner who is thereby damned. Not only that: her downfall is brought about in part by the glimmerings of a good instinct in her behaviour towards Joas.

Yet paradoxically it is perhaps in the harshness of his view of the relationship between God and humanity that Racine, in depicting the wicked Athalie, seems to me to show that ultimate sympathy for human beings and for their plight which is the hallmark of the truly great writer. He must have realised when writing his play that, although it was written ostensibly for the edification of believers, the members of his Court audience would be of differing degrees of Christian commitment — some deeply committed, some lukewarm and some more than sceptical — and that his play would prove over the years to be divisive, some seeing it from one point of view, others from another.

It is, then, a great tribute to its author that, from whichever angle the play is viewed, it shows us human beings, with all their virtues and faults, being put to the test in extreme circumstances. The story of Athalie, first apparently triumphant, then dashed in a tragic fall, indeed fills us all with pity and fear, as Aristotle decreed that tragedy should, and reminds us of the frailty of our human nature. There can be few whom the spectacle of this fellow creature going to her grim death can leave unmoved, even though they know how she would have treated her opponents, and the child Joas in particular, had she won.

One of the play's broader lessons is surely, then, that human beings are highly complex and fascinating in their beliefs, their characters and their conduct. The wicked Athalie does show some traces of good, however transitory; the prophet Joad shows a harshness which few Christians nowadays would consider exemplary. Both characters form part of a human race which shows a seemingly endless variety of possibilities in its behaviour, and which seventeenth-century writers, *moralistes* like La Rochefoucauld and La Bruyère, playwrights like Corneille, Racine and Molière, novelists like Mme de La Fayette and many other authors, made it their business to explore.

The exploration is not, however, that of the butterfly-hunter, content to pin his specimens in a glass case for the curious to inspect. Its basis is not merely intellectual, although the intellect guarantees a sufficient detachment from excessive, blinding emotionalism. It also involves the heart — Racine's declared aim in the theatre was 'plaire et toucher' — and, as has been suggested, an ultimate sympathy for the writer's fellow-creatures which is transmitted to the audience: Athalie's fate touches us deeply, not because we forget her evil deeds, but because we recognise her as being like ourselves, a fellow member of fallen humanity. Moreover, Racine's exploration of human nature in *Athalie* is conducted by means of the most magnificent, musical and subtle poetry. Both by its poetic form and by its content *Athalie* is a work of art which stands amongst the highest summits ever attained in French, and indeed in world, literature.

Appendix: Jansenism — a Note

The Jansenist movement was mentioned at the beginning of this book and compared to the Puritan movement in Britain. Since its influence is, I believe, important, indeed crucial to the interpretation of *Athalie*, a little more detail about it may be helpful.

France in Racine's time professed to be a Christian country. The vast majority of its inhabitants were, to a greater or lesser degree, believing and practising Christians and most were, like Racine, Catholics. Theological arguments were frequent within the Catholic Church, and had been centred, particularly earlier in the century, around the nature and extent of people's responsibility for their own actions — a subject with obvious relevance to the theatre, both then and now.

We are all conscious of the fact that we do not always carry out our good intentions. As St Paul says (Romans 7.15), 'I cannot understand my own behaviour. I fail to carry out the things I want to do, and I find myself doing the very things I hate.' It is standard Christian teaching that to avoid evil and do good we need help from some source outside ourselves: that source is God and the help, since it is given freely (Latin *gratis*) is called grace (Latin *gratia*). At the same time, however, we also have Free Will — we are free, at least to some extent, to choose how we behave and are thus, to that extent, responsible for our actions.

However, since God is all-powerful, it is inconceivable that His grace will not accomplish its ends: to use the theological jargon of the time, grace, when it is brought into action, will be efficacious (*grâce efficace*). But what then becomes of Free Will? Does it keep its independence and have a role to play or is it swamped by the all-powerful grace of the all-powerful God?

Many attempts were made by theologians to resolve this dilemma. Those who were perhaps the wisest recommended that since the problem was a mystery beyond human comprehension, people ought to spend their time in trying to use grace rather than in trying to define it. Others, however, brought out theories aimed at solving the problem and this, inevitably, led to bitter disputes, which came to a head towards the middle of the century. The main contestants were the theologians of the Jesuit order and those of the Jansenists, a name given by their opponents to the followers of Bishop Janssen of Ypres, who had died in 1638.

The Jesuits emphasised the role of Free Will: God always offers us His grace ('My grace is sufficient for you', II Cor. 12.9) — whence the jargon term for this offered grace: sufficient grace (*grâce suffisante*) — but he wants us to give our consent and/or co-operation before it takes effect or, in the jargon, becomes efficacious (*efficace*). A chemist might express it thus:

Sufficient Grace + Free Will → Efficacious Grace

For the Jansenists on the other hand, who were centred around the abbey of Port-Royal, where Racine received most of his education, God gives His grace to whomsoever and whenever He wants and grace needs no human consent or co-operation to become *efficace*. While not denying the existence of Free Will, at least in theory, the Jansenist view of human nature was that it was so weak and corrupt in itself as to be incapable of making any useful response to God.

Their opponents made the obvious objections: if one accepts the Jansenist view of the problem, Free Will becomes meaningless and God's choice of who will be saved, and who not, appears totally arbitrary. Moreover, good or bad behaviour becomes irrelevant, since it cannot change our fate. The reason why wicked people, such as Athalie, are wicked is that they have been refused grace and are thus destined, indeed predestined before birth, to eternal punishment by the divine will or whim. Such a seemingly capricious deity recalls Gloucester's lines in *King Lear* (IV.1):

As flies to wanton boys are we to the Gods:
They kill us for their sport.

It would be unfair, however, to view the Jansenists as inhuman fanatics. They would, no doubt, have rejected my representation of the conclusions to be drawn from their views as unfair, although it is not, I believe, an unfair representation of the spirit of their beliefs. What in fact concerned them in practice was not the logical conclusions to be drawn from their doctrines but the consciousness, drawn from practical experience, of man's weakness and sinfulness in comparison with the enormous power and majesty of God. It was, in other words, a question of where to put the emphasis in the relationship between man and God, and this in turn depended on one's image of God.

Modern Christians, in the Western world at least, reflecting the ideas of their own time and place, tend to see God as a friend, as a Father always ready to love and forgive. In Racine's day, too, people must have seen God in terms of their own time and place, but since theirs was a hierarchical age, an age of absolute rulers, it was perhaps natural for them to see God as a kind of super-king, an awesome judge and monarch, the God of might and majesty before whom all trembled, and although they knew Him also to be the God of love, fear was perhaps the instinctive reaction both in Jansenist and in other circles towards the Almighty. There were, however, others in the century who viewed God very differently, and the love, rather than the fear, of God pervaded the teachings of St François de Sales and St Vincent de Paul, two of the most influential figures in the Church earlier in the century.

The Jansenists were persecuted during the later part of Louis XIV's reign and their doctrines (or supposed doctrines) were condemned by the Pope in 1713 just as the doctrines of Calvin, an even more radical upholder of the idea of Predestination to salvation or damnation, had been condemned over a hundred years before. Yet Jansenist influence has been widespread in France and elsewhere even till recent times, and not always a healthy influence, as François Mauriac, amongst others, has shown both through his fictional characters and in other writings, notably in his biography of Racine.

Such a doctrine as Jansenism may seem strange, even incomprehensible, for most young people brought up in the modern western world, whose normal expectations of what life may offer in material terms would have seemed incredible even to the richest in Racine's time: survival to seventy or more, freedom from most diseases, starvation virtually unheard of, comfort for the majority and many means of distraction at hand to save them from thinking of the great unmentionable, death. Racine, however, lived in a Third World-type country. Half the population died before reaching twenty, disease was rampant, painkillers (alcohol apart) unknown and death ever present and audibly so, as Donne's famous line reminds us: '...never send to know for whom the bell tolls; it tolls for thee'. Life for the majority was, as Hobbes, another contemporary, put it, 'nasty, brutish and short'.

To live in such conditions must have led to different perspectives from those which prevail for most of us. Some people no doubt reacted by following the philosophy of 'gather ye rosebuds while ye may'; others, faced with the likelihood of not living long, became very conscious and fearful of what lay beyond death and deemed it prudent to make urgent preparations for meeting their Maker. The Jansenist view of God was, as has been noted, a rather particular one, but the narrowness of mental vision which characterises most human beings — we are incapable of seizing the whole breadth of the picture before us but tend to see only certain aspects of it — is apt to make us all tend towards extremes. Thus the sense of their own nothingness beside the Almighty was likely, I believe, to lead the Jansenists to the kind of narrow views which they held and which were reinforced by the persecutions to which they were subjected. This explanation is clearly very incomplete and simplistic, but it may be helpful for readers who might otherwise remain mystified by Jansenism and the reasons for the extraordinary power of its influence, not least in relation to *Athalie*.

Select Bibliography

Bibliographical Works

1. Cabeen, D.C., and Brody, J., *A Critical Bibliography of French Literature* (Syracuse, N.Y.), Vol. III, edited by N. Edelman (1961), and Vol. III A (Supplement), edited by H.G. Hall (1983), is the most recent critical bibliography for the seventeenth century, giving summaries of the works it mentions and devoting a great deal of space to Racine. For details of works published since 1983 see the appropriate section of 2.
2. *The Year's Work in Modern Language Studies*, published annually (in London) by the Modern Humanities Research Association.

Editions of Racine

3. *Œuvres complètes*, edited by R. Picard, 2 vols, Bibliothèque de la Pléiade (Paris: Gallimard, 1951–52), is the current standard edition.
4. *Œuvres complètes*, edited by P. Mesnard, Les Grands Ecrivains de la France, 8 vols plus two albums (Paris: Hachette, 1865–73), which 3 was intended to replace, nonetheless remains valuable. Of the albums, one is devoted to iconography and the other to musical scores, including Moreau's score for *Athalie*.
5. *Œuvres complètes*, with a preface by P. Clarac, Collection L'Intégrale (Paris: Seuil, 1962), is a useful and affordable one-volume edition.

Editions of 'Athalie'

The French school editions, published by Bordas, Larousse etc. are good value and contain much useful material in the form of notes and background.
6. *Athalie*, edited by R.-Y. Le Mazou, Collection Univers des Lettres (Paris: Bordas, 1962) contains, among other things, extracts from Racine's sources, notably the Bible and Bossuet (*9* below).
7. *Athalie*, ed. P. France (Oxford University Press, 1966) has a helpful introduction and notes.

Sources

8. *The Jerusalem Bible* (London: Darton, Longman and Todd, 1966).
9. Bossuet, J.-B. *Discours sur l'histoire universelle* (Paris: Firmin-Didot, 1864). The *sixième époque*, pp.20–22 in this edition, contains the relevant passage.
10. Garnier, R., *Les Juifves*, in *Œuvres complètes*, ed. R. Lebègue (Paris: Les Belles Lettres, 1949).

Background to the French Classical Theatre

11. Adam, A., *Grandeur and Illusion: French Literature and Society 1600–1715* (London: Penguin, 1974) is a useful general introduction to the century.
12. Aristotle, *On the Art of Poetry* (the *Poetics*) in *Classical Literary Criticism*, trans. T.S. Dorsch, Penguin Books, 1965.
13. Bray, R., *La Formation de la doctrine classique en France* (Paris: Hachette, 1927; Nizet, 1957), is a large and authoritative work.
14. Brereton, G., *French Tragic Drama in the 16th and 17th Centuries* (London: Methuen, 1973), is a useful introduction to its subject.
15. Lough, J., *Seventeenth-Century French Drama: the Background* (Oxford: Clarendon Press, 1979). Good on practical matters.
16. W.G. Moore, *French Classical Literature, an Essay* (Oxford: OUP, 1961).
17. —, *Racine's 'Britannicus'*, Studies in French Literature (London: Arnold, 1960). These two short books are very helpful for the beginner, as regards both the classical theatre in general and Racine in particular.
18. Scherer, J., *La Dramaturgie classique en France* (Paris: Nizet, 1959), like Bray (*13*), is monumental and authoritative.

Works about Racine and 'Athalie'

The number of books and articles about Racine is enormous, and they cover a wide range of viewpoints. The titles which follow represent a very small selection of more 'traditional' works.
19. Adam, A., *Histoire de la littérature française au dix-septième siècle*, 5 vols (Paris: Domat, 1948–56), is still the standard work on the literary history of the century. Vol. 5 covers the period of *Athalie* and contains useful criticism as well as background, taking a sympathetic view of the main character.

20. Butler, P., *Racine: a Study* (London: Heinemann, 1974), is a short introduction to the author and his work and has some good pages on *Athalie*.

21. Cambier, M., *Racine et Mme de Maintenon: 'Esther' et 'Athalie' à Saint-Cyr* (Brussels: Durendal; Paris: Lethielleux, 1949), is more concerned with background than with criticism.

21a. Campbell, J., is the author of two articles, 'The God of *Athalie*', in *French Studies*, No.43, 1989, pp.385–404 and 'The Exposition of *Athalie*', in *Seventeenth-Century French Studies*, No.12, 1990, pp.149–57.

22. Chédozeau, B., 'Le Tragique d'*Athalie*', is an article in the *Revue d'Histoire Littéraire de la France* for 1967 (pp.494–501). The author sees Racine's tragic vision in *Athalie* as new, because of its perspectives on the past and the future.

23. Descotes, M., *Les Grands Rôles du théâtre de Racine* (Paris: PUF, 1957), has an interesting chapter on acting the parts of Athalie and of Joad.

23a. Forman, E.B. (ed.), *Racine: Appraisal & Re-appraisal* (University of Bristol, 1991), contains, among other items, an article by J. Trethewey on biblical and classical elements in *Athalie*.

24. Ginestier, P., 'La Problématique d'Athalie', an article in the *Newsletter of the Society for Seventeenth-Century French Studies*, 5 (1983), brings out the ambiguities of the play, with a close commentary on the text, and insists on the importance of the fact that the play was written to be acted.

25. Hubert, J.D., *Essai d'exégèse racinienne* (Paris: Nizet, 1956), has a valuable section on *Athalie*.

26. Knight, R.C., *Racine et la Grèce* (Paris: Boivin, 1950; Nizet, 1974) has a chapter on 'Les tragédies sacrées' which details the Greek sources of, and Greek influences on, *Athalie*.

27. Lancaster, H.C., *A History of French Dramatic Literature in the Seventeenth Century*, Part IV, Vol. 1 (Baltimore: Johns Hopkins U.P., 1940), is part of a vast and magnificent work which details every play written in the period. It has a particularly full and helpful section on *Athalie* and its background.

28. Lapp, J.C., *Aspects of Racinian Tragedy* (Toronto: University of Toronto, 1956), is an attempt to define the essence of tragedy in Racine.

29. Loukovitch, K., *L'Evolution de la tragédie religieuse en France* (Paris: Droz, 1933), sees *Athalie* in the context of the development of this genre from the Renaissance to the end of the seventeenth century.

29a. Maskell, D., *Racine: a theatrical reading* (Oxford, Clarendon Press, 1991), examines Racine's stagecraft and use of visual language and contains much of interest on *Athalie*.

30. Maulnier, T., *Racine* (Paris: Gallimard, 1935), sees *Athalie* as a Christian tragedy, which by its religious character is a microcosm of the Christian belief that resurrection follows death (cf. the 'rebirth' of Joas and the future coming of the Messiah in spite of all human failings), and renews the link with the religious tradition of the Greek theatre, noting that the latter was consecrated to Dionysos, a god who died and was born again.

31. Mauriac, F., *Racine* (Paris: Plon, 1928), gives a novelist's insight, clearly drawn from personal experience, into the influence of Jansenism on the mind and outlook of Racine. Good on *Athalie*.

32. Mercanton, J., *Racine*, Les Ecrivains devant Dieu (Paris: Desclée de Brouwer, 1966), has some pages on *Athalie*.

33. Mongrédien, G., *'Athalie' de Racine* (Paris: Malfère, 1929), is a study of the background to the play rather than of the play itself, but is none the less interesting.

34. Moore, W.G., *The Classical Drama of France* (Oxford University Press, 1971), has some illuminating pages on *Athalie* as well as being an excellent introduction to the wider subject.

35. Moreau, P., *Racine, l'homme et l'œuvre*, Connaissance des Lettres (Paris: Boivin, 1943; Hatier, 1952), is a good general study of Racine.

36. Mourgues, O. de, *Racine or the Triumph of Relevance* (Cambridge University Press, 1967), is a clear, subtle, sensitive and beautifully written analysis of Racinian tragedy. Highly recommended.

37. Orcibal, J., *La Genèse d''Esther' et d''Athalie'* (Paris: Vrin, 1950), is a work by a very fine scholar whose ingenious but unconvincing view of *Athalie* as a *pièce à clé*, with a propaganda function aimed at supporting the cause of the deposed James II of England, can distract the reader from some very helpful material, particularly in the later part of the book, about the role of Providence in the play.

38. Picard, R., *La Carrière de Jean Racine* (Paris: Gallimard, 1956). Long, fascinating and very solidly documented; sees Racine as an orphan who made a highly successful career for himself through the theatre but returned towards the end of his life to the faith of his childhood. Particularly interesting as answering Orcibal's 'Jacobite' view of *Athalie*.

39. —, *Nouveau corpus racinianum* (Paris: CNRS, 1971). An invaluable work which gives all the references to Racine during the seventeenth century in chronological order (an update of an earlier edition).

40. Pocock, G., *Corneille and Racine* (Cambridge University Press, 1973), is concerned with tragic form in the two authors and has some excellent pages on *Athalie*.

40a. Rohou, J., *Jean Racine entre sa carrière, son œuvre et Dieu* (Paris, Fayard, 1992), following on from Picard (*38* above), sets out to resolve some of the contradictions in Racine's life.

41. Sainte-Beuve, Ch., *Histoire de Port-Royal*, edited by M. Leroy, Bibliothèque de la Pléiade (Paris: Gallimard, 1957), vol. 3 (VI, 11, 585–93), has some illuminating pages on *Athalie*, notably maintaining that the main character is one who never makes an appearance —God. The original edition dates from 1857.

42. Spillebout, G., *Le Vocabulaire biblique dans les tragédies sacrées de Racine* (Geneva: Droz, 1968), is an interesting study of the language of *Esther* and *Athalie*.

43. Taphanel, A., *Le Théâtre de Saint-Cyr (1689–1792), d'après des documents inédits* (Paris: Baudry, 1876).

44. — (ed.), *Mémoires de Manseau, intendant à la maison royale de Saint-Cyr* (Versailles: Bernard, 1902). This and *41* give important sources for the circumstances of performance, etc. of *Esther* and *Athalie*.

45. Turnell, M., *The Classical Moment* (London: Hamish Hamilton, 1947), has a chapter on *Athalie*.

46. Voltaire, *Œuvres complètes* (Paris: Firmin Didot, 1862), Vol. 2, p.131, contains his *Discours historique et critique à l'occasion de la tragédie des 'Guèbres'*.

47. Yarrow, P., *Racine* (Oxford: Blackwell, 1978), is a useful general study of Racine with a section on *Athalie*.

A number of works have appeared over the last thirty years or so which view Racine from less traditional angles. The best known are, in chronological order, as follows.

48. Goldmann, L., *Le Dieu caché* (Paris: Gallimard, 1956), gives a Marxist analysis of Racine and the Jansenist influences on him.

49. Mauron, C., *L'Inconscient dans l'œuvre et la vie de Racine* (Aix-en-Provence: Publications des Annales de la Faculté des Lettres, 1957), sets out to apply the techniques of psychoanalysis to the study of Racine and his works.

50. Barthes, R., *Sur Racine* (Paris, 1963) follows the psychoanalytical approach in more radical style, launching what came to be known as *La Nouvelle Critique*. This began a virtual critics' war by somewhat provocatively rejecting the traditional 'historical' approach in favour of what the defenders of the latter, notably Picard, R., in *Nouvelle*

Critique ou nouvelle imposture (Paris, 1965) attacked with equal vigour as being mere subjectivism.

On Jansenism

51. *The New Catholic Encyclopedia*, vol. VII (New York: McGraw-Hill, 1967) contains useful short articles by L. Cognet on 'Jansenism' (p.820) and by B. Matteuci on 'Jansenistic Piety' (p.824).
52. Cognet, L., *Le Jansénisme*, Coll. Que sais-je?, 960 (Paris: PUF, 1964), is a short and authoritative introduction to this complex subject.

CRITICAL GUIDES TO FRENCH TEXTS

edited by
Roger Little, Wolfgang van Emden, David Williams